SCRAP PATCHWORK

Traditionally Modern Quilts

Organize Your Stash to Tell Your Color Story

SANDRA CLEMONS

stashBOOKS.

an imprint of C&T Publishing

Publisher: Amy Marson

Creative Director: Gailen Runge

Art Director/Cover Designer: Kristy Zacharias

Editor: Monica Gyulai

Technical Editors: Nan Powell and Amanda Siegfried

Book Design: Page + Pixel

Production Coordinator: Zinnia Heinzmann

Production Editors: Alice Mace Nakanishi and Jessie Brotman

Illustrator: Kirstie L. Pettersen

Photo Assistant: Sarah Frost

Style photography by Page + Pixel and instructional photography by Diane Pedersen, unless otherwise noted

Published by Stash Books, an imprint of C&T Publishing, Inc., P.O. Box 1456, Lafayette, CA 94549

Library of Congress Cataloging-in-Publication Data

Names: Clemons, Sandra, 1979-

Title: Scrap patchwork : traditionally modern quilts-organize your stash to tell your color story / Sandra Clemons.

Description: Lafayette, California : C&T Publishing, [2016]

Identifiers: LCCN 2015025191 | ISBN 9781617451423 (soft cover)

Subjects: LCSH: Patchwork quilts. | Patchwork--Patterns.

Classification: LCC TT835 .C59526 2016 | DDC 746.46--dc23

LC record available at http://lccn.loc.gov/2015025191

Printed in China

10 9 8 7 6 5 4 3 2 1

DEDICATION

To Garrett:

"Two are better than one, because they have a good return for their work: If one falls down, his friend can help him up. But pity the man who falls and has no one to help him up!"
—Ecclesiastes 4:9–10

ACKNOWLEDGMENTS

I wish to thank the following people for their support, encouragement, knowledge, and inspiration:

My husband, who took on more chores around the house, kept me fed, and made sure I was getting enough sleep. I love you more than words can ever express. Thank you for always being there for me, no matter what. We did it.

My three-year-old daughter, Audrey, whose willingness to give up a lot of our crafting, reading, and exploring time really helped me with this book. I hope you are proud of me. I love you.

My parents, who taught me that through preparation, hard work and focus, goals can be accomplished. My in-laws, who shared their inspiring family quilts and pushed me to turn my hobby into a business.

My handsome Bernese mountain dog, Harvey, who passed away during the writing of this book. He was my running partner and silent companion and always sat near my feet when I sewed. I miss seeing your fur in my work, buddy.

The rest of my family and friends—both in my old hood of Rock Island, Illinois, and in Denver, Colorado. All of you hold a special place in my heart.

All the quilters I have met along the way, especially the Longmont Quilt Guild Retreaters, Great American Quilt Factory staff, and Denver Quilt Guild. Thank you for your inspiration and friendship.

My church family throughout the years: Grace Korean Church, Bethel Assembly of God Church, University Hills Baptist Church, Mississippi Avenue Baptist Church, and Harvest Bible Chapel. Thank you for your fellowship and knowledge as I grew in my faith.

Most important, I thank God for blessing me with this opportunity.

contents

introduction

It's no secret that quilters love fabric. Many of us start our first quilts by purchasing fabric as needed for particular patterns. Some of us dive right into building a stash. Eventually, all of us end up with unused yardage and leftover pieces stowed for future use.

The thirteen fabulous quilts in this book were designed to make use of scraps. While many of the quilts rely on large pieces of neutral fabric to achieve a clean, modern look, they also include a range of colorful fabrics that pop. Dig into your own stash for these scrappy elements and make these designs your own. Each project includes design notes so that you can get the same look and feel when choosing fabrics from your own collection or the local quilt shop.

While scraps are useful, they have a way of piling up. In Organizing Scraps and Stash Fabrics (page 13), you will learn the best methods for storing and organizing your scraps, building your stash, and narrowing down fabric choices to make beautiful quilts.

Understanding color is important for both sorting your stash and selecting fabrics for quiltmaking. In Color Basics (page 5), you will learn how to get the look and feel you want in a quilt by choosing the right kind of color scheme.

These scrappy, modern quilt designs are geared toward beginning and intermediate quilters. Step-by-step instructions and special methods explained in Special Techniques (page 103) make it easy to get things right the first time, with minimal waste and simple assembly.

These bright and clean designs rely on traditional elements, including classic block designs, structure, and traditional workmanship. But they also have a modern feel, due to their use of solids and textured fabrics, large blocks, and bright colors combined in fresh ways.

I started quilting ten years ago and have been hooked on the art form ever since. I hope you will enjoy the process of making these quilts as much as I did and become inspired to make a treasure of your own.

Sandra P. Clemons
sandraclemons.blogspot.com

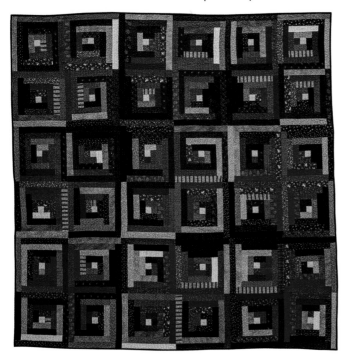

My first quilt, a Log Cabin design that measured 120″ × 120″

COLOR BASICS

Part of the fun in quiltmaking is selecting colors and fabrics. However, this step can sometimes be overwhelming and intimidating, especially when working with scraps. Understanding how color and fabric choices affect a quilt's overall appearance makes choosing fabrics more enjoyable.

Thinking About Color

When thinking about colors, some people look to the color wheel for ideas and planning. It shows how colors relate to each other and helps identify why certain combinations are pleasing to the eye.

There are also colors that you don't see on the basic color wheel—tints, tones, and shades. These variations of colors are lighter (tints), darker (shades), and muted (tones). Some of these variations fall into the category of neutrals.

And then there are white and black. Whites can brighten areas, and blacks can anchor a design. When used together, they are the ultimate in contrast and movement—probably your lightest light and the darkest dark.

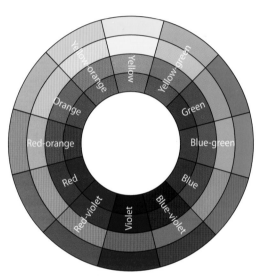

The color wheel

color messages

Colors deliver messages to us even when we don't realize it. Some colors are calming, while others rev us up. There is much discussion about what colors "mean," but here are some common associations. When you choose a palette for a quilt, keep in mind how you want it to make people feel.

RED: energy, strength, power, passion, and love

PINK: romance, friendship, grace, and femininity

ORANGE: joy, attraction, encouragement, trust, and enthusiasm

YELLOW: happiness, sunshine, freshness, youth, and intellect

GREEN: harmony, safety, and nature

AQUA: healing and protection

BLUE: depth, peace, and sincerity

PURPLE: royalty, power, luxury, and mysticism

WHITE: light, goodness, and purity

BLACK: elegance, formality, mystery, and power

BROWN: masculinity and stability

VALUE AND CONTRAST

Before discussing color, we need to talk about value and contrast. *Value* is the relative lightness or darkness of a color/fabric. *Contrast* is the difference between colors/fabrics. Contrast makes patterns or designs stand out. Contrast of value makes the strongest impression.

Contrast and value are relative. A fabric may look dark when it is next to a light fabric and look light when it is next to a dark fabric. If you aren't sure whether your fabrics have enough contrast, use your handy-dandy phone or camera to snap a black-and-white photo as you play with choices to see which fabrics stand out and which sit back. Do you have the contrast you want? Is one fabric too strong or too weak? I take a photo with my phone to confirm my choices for the depth of contrast.

In this block from *Meadows* (page 57), the "medium" orange fabric is light when next to dark teal or dark orange, but it is dark when next to the light background.

TIP

Decoding Color

The Ultimate 3-in-1 Color Tool (by C&T Publishing) is a handy reference when trying to make sense of color and value when planning out quilts. Take it when you go shopping to help buy the right fabrics for your chosen scheme.

COLOR RELATIONSHIPS

There are a number of "official" color schemes, but when using fabric (especially multicolored prints) and particularly when using scraps, it can sometimes be hard to stick to a specific, formal color scheme. Instead, I think it is most helpful to understand how colors work in general and then use those principles as you select fabric for your quilts. Even if you don't use the exact correct colors for the color scheme, you'll get the color relationship effects.

Warm and Cool Colors

The color wheel can be divided into warm and cool colors. Warm colors are the reds, oranges, and yellows. They are vivid, create energy, and tend to pop. Cool colors are greens, blues, and violets. They are calming and relaxing and tend to recede.

The warm stars in *Magic* (page 86) leap out from the cool blue background.

TIP

Pay particular attention to yellow when planning quilt designs. Yellow is full of energy and is the first place your eyes land. It can be the strongest, most dominant color in a design, even if it's used more sparingly than other colors.

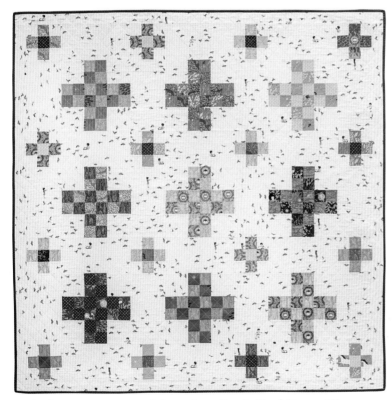

Notice how your eye goes right to the yellow in *Playful* (page 40).

Calming Color Schemes

Using one color (monochromatic) or several colors that are next to each other on the color wheel (analogous) usually creates a sense of unity, serenity, and comfort. Quilts made this way are pleasant and can convey the feeling of the main color, whether warm or cool. Contrast is the key to making these color schemes interesting. Include a mix of light and dark versions of the chosen color(s) to create depth, dimension, and interest. Mixing small- and large-scale prints also adds contrast.

Twilight (page 33) uses an analogous color scheme in red-violet to violet to blue.

TIP

Want to Take These Quilts Up a Notch?

Calming quilts are calm because there is limited contrast. It you want to make these quilts a little more exciting, add a pop of contrast in either color or value.

Using low-volume or low-contrast fabrics is another way to make a calming quilt. These quilts generally use fabrics with whites and soft colors.

A quilt made using only neutrals can result in a very calming quilt.

Harmonious Color Schemes

Using colors that are spaced around the color wheel can create interesting and energetic yet harmonious palettes. Try using one color as the quilt's main focus and the other colors as accents. Fabric choices should vary among tints, tones, and shades to make sure there is value contrast. Using a neutral background will add dimension by making your colors stand out.

Three evenly spaced colors are called triadic, four colors in a rectangle shape are often called double complementary, and four colors in a square shape are called quadratic or tetradic.

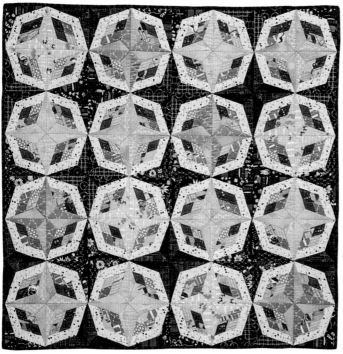

Magic (page 86) uses a triadic color scheme of blue, yellow, and tints and tones of red.

RIGHT: *Bracelet* (page 51) uses a double-complementary color scheme with blues and oranges, red-violets, and yellow-greens.

Exciting Color Schemes

Using colors that are across from each other on the color wheel creates the most vibrant and energetic color palettes. You can use colors that are directly across from each other (complementary) or colors that are adjacent to one of the complementary colors (split complementary).

As with harmonious color palettes, it's important to make one color dominant and to use the others more sparingly, as a highlight or accent; using a neutral background will make your color stand out.

 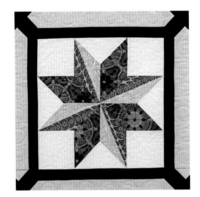 

Crossroads (page 79) includes blocks with complementary pairs that make for exciting color combinations.

TIP
Still Having Trouble Selecting Fabrics for a Quilt?

Sometimes the best color schemes start with a piece of beautiful, multicolored fabric that you love. You can build your quilt using the colors within it. An easy way to see the hues used in your fabric is to look at the fabric's selvage. Along one edge of the fabric, you will often find dots of the colors used in the print. Use these dots as inspiration for your color palette. You don't need to use all the colors or match them exactly. Slight shifts in color will enhance your quilt.

Rainbow Color Schemes

A rainbow color scheme uses all or most of the colors on the color wheel. Rainbow quilts are often bright and happy.

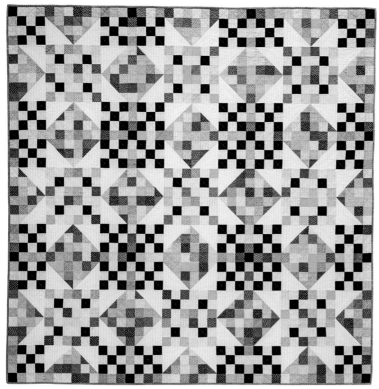

Fiddlestars (page 45) has a rainbow color scheme.

TIP

Photocopy the Quilt Design

Hesitant about your color selection? Photocopy your quilt design in black-and-white ink only. If the printer allows, select a low-contrast or draft setting. Color in the design with colored pencils or markers to audition schemes.

color inspiration binder

If you want to create your own palettes, start keeping a color inspiration binder to use when planning your next stellar quilt.

Any time you see a pretty object or image, take a photo or clip the page and save it in your color binder. Often, my color inspiration comes from photos I've taken out in nature. But a flower bouquet, magazine clipping, or the latest fashion trends can be just as inspiring. When selecting color palettes from photographs or magazine clippings, add neutrals and include contrasting fabrics to add dimension to your quilts.

scale

The scale or size of a print can have an important effect on a quilt's design. When I first started quilting, my quilts didn't show much movement, because I loved selecting small-scale prints. This resulted in boring and uninteresting quilts.

On the other hand, using just large-scale prints would result in a quilt so busy that your eye wouldn't be able to rest and enjoy the quilt's craftsmanship. To add movement and interest to quilts, include a variety of small-, medium-, and large-scale prints. Another way to add movement is to mix up prints with solid, floral, directional, and geometric fabrics. Sometimes I'll add a cute novelty print.

Although solids are popular in quilting, they do make quilts seem flat. Just make sure you choose fabrics that achieve the look you want.

ORGANIZING SCRAPS AND STASH FABRICS

When your fabric is neatly organized, it's easy to evaluate all the wonderful options you already have for future quilt projects. I've tried many organizing systems over the years, but the one I explain in this chapter has stayed with me because it's simple to maintain.

Folding Fabric

I fold all my fabric pieces—big and small—so they end up having the same dimensions, which makes the pieces easy to stack. I try my best to fold raw edges to the inside.

FOLDING A FAT QUARTER

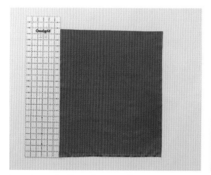

Lay lengthwise along ruler.

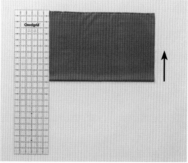

Fold in half lengthwise.

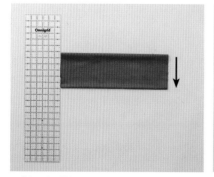

Fold in half lengthwise again.

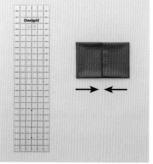

Fold in from both sides.

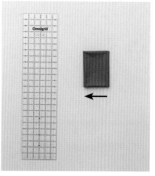

Fold in half.

FOLDING A HALF-YARD

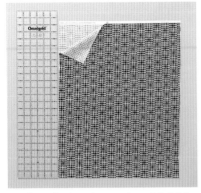

Lay lengthwise along ruler with fold toward you.

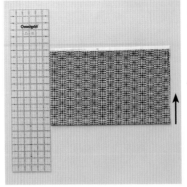

Fold in half lengthwise.

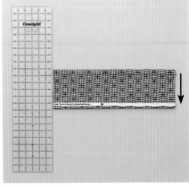

Fold in half lengthwise again.

FOLDING TWO YARDS

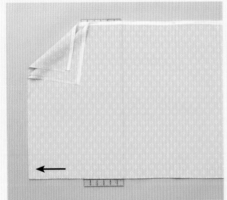

Lay lengthwise along ruler with fold toward you. Fold in half by the length of fabric.

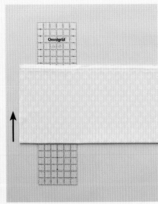

Fold in half lengthwise.

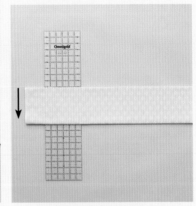

Fold in half lengthwise again.

FOLDING MORE THAN TWO YARDS

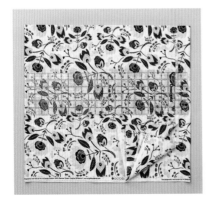

Lay lengthwise with fold away from you.

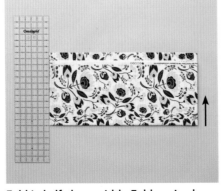

Fold in half along width. Fold again along width. Fabric is now about 11˝ tall.

Place ruler on right side of fabric and fold fabric around ruler.

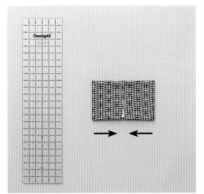 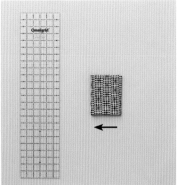

Fold in from both sides. **Fold in half.**

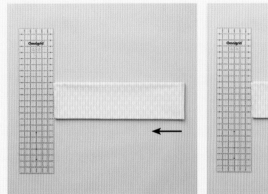  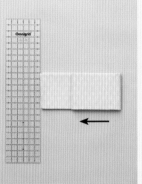 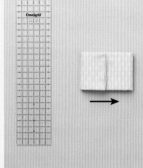 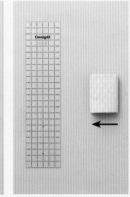

Fold in half. **Fold over two-thirds.** **Fold over one-third.** **Fold in half.**

For clean finish, fold end in. **Finish folding.** **When folded as shown, fabric pieces of different sizes can still be neatly stacked.**

Fabric's Overall Color

With fabric neatly folded, it's time to determine the overall color of each piece. I sort and store my fabric in color-wheel order because it's pleasing to the eye and makes it easy to see any gaps in my collection that I may want to fill on shopping trips.

In addition to pieces of fabric that are clearly one color, there are mixed prints and designs that can be harder to classify. Here are some guidelines on what to look for when categorizing multicolored fabric:

- **Tone-on-tone** fabrics consist of primarily one color.

- **White-on-color** fabrics are made of a color fabric with a print outlined in white. Generally the color is much more dominant, and the white is an outline of the design.

- **Small-scale** fabrics generally have a strong background color with a small-scale print of multiple colors. When standing away from the fabric, you'll see one dominant color more clearly.

- **Large-scale** fabrics are similar to small-scale fabrics, but the print is large in scale—and yet a background color can still be determined.

- **Multicolored** fabrics are the most difficult to decipher a main color. These large-scale prints have many colors, making it difficult to decide the background color. Many times, these fabrics are a great background or backing fabric, or they can be used as a large border or for building a color palette for your quilt.

Storing Stash and Scrap Fabric

There are many ways to store stash and scrap fabric—open shelving, cubbies, drawers, boxes, clear plastic bins, closet organizers, zipping plastic bags, and mini bolts are all good options. I'll explain how I store my stash and scraps and why I like this system.

Stash fabric is any piece that is a quarter-yard (including a fat quarter) or bigger. Scrap fabric is anything smaller.

STASH FABRIC STORAGE

I store my fabric on open shelves or in cubbies because I enjoy seeing my fabric all at once. I am also inspired by the colors when planning projects. Although plastic bins and drawers hide fabric from easy viewing, they also protect it from sunlight and fading, which can make them a smart choice. When fabric is stored out of sight, however, it's hidden and, worse, easy to forget when it's time to build a quilt.

When storing your fabric, try to keep it out of direct sunlight to prevent fading over time. Also, try to store your fabric in a single layer to take away the need to move and shift fabric around or, worse, forget about it. For humid climates, avoid storing fabric in plastic, as moisture can get trapped inside, causing mildew.

I sort and store fabric by color wheel. I also do my best to break down multicolored bundles. Although bundles look great tied together, there is a better chance of getting more interesting palettes out of your stash if you intermix these pieces. Does the idea of breaking up those coordinated bundles force you out of your comfort zone? Trust me—you will put together great fabric combinations this way!

For each color, I start with lights to darks, finishing with large scale or multicolored fabrics. In addition to color sorting, I also have separate storage for my reproduction, Japanese, and linen fabrics.

fabric storage boxes

Finished box: 9½˝ × 12½˝ × 9½˝

Fabric storage box

These fabric boxes are great! They can be used for storing stash or scrap fabric. The color of each box represents the colors of the scraps inside. I used Mochi Dot Linen by Moda, because it comes in many colors.

TIP

Mix-and-match fat quarters are fun to use for this project!

Fabric Requirements

Exterior interfacing: ½ yard stiff fusible interfacing, such as fast2fuse Heavy (by C&T Publishing) or Pellon 71F Peltex

Interior fabric: ½ yard

Exterior fabric: ½ yard

Cutting Instructions

FABRIC AND INTERFACING:

For exterior interfacing, cut 2 pieces 18˝ × 20˝.

For interior fabric, cut 2 pieces 18˝ × 20˝.

For exterior fabric, cut 2 pieces 18˝ × 20˝.

BOX CONSTRUCTION

Use ½˝ seam allowances.

1. Press the interfacing to the wrong side of the exterior fabric, following the manufacturer's instructions.

2. For each of the exterior pieces and each of the interior fabric pieces, cut a 4½˝ square notch from both bottom corners. **FIG. A**

3. For the front and back exteriors, stitch the sides and bottom together, right sides facing. Do the same for the interior. Do not sew the notches or the top of the box.

4. Press the seams open.

5. For both the exterior and interior, square the bottom of the box by aligning the side seam with the bottom seam. Stitch across. Repeat this step for all 4 corners. FIG. B & C

6. Insert the box's exterior inside the box's interior with right sides together.

7. Stitch around the top edge of the box, leaving an opening of about 4˝.

8. Turn the box right side out through the opening. Push the interior into the box.

9. Fold back the seam allowance of the opening. Pin it in place.

10. Topstitch around the top edge of the box.

11. Fold over the top of the box if you like. FIG. D

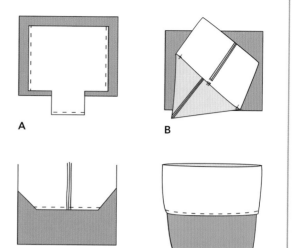

SCRAP FABRIC STORAGE

As with bigger fabric pieces, I organize my scraps by color because that's how I will look through them when I need just the right piece for a quilt.

Organizing by size is another option. People who prefer to organize by size set up bins for pieces that measure 1½˝, 2˝, 2½˝, and larger than 2½˝. Personally, I lose track of pieces when I organize by size, which is why I prefer to organize by color.

I store scraps in color-coded Fabric Storage Boxes (left). This system makes it is so easy

for me to use my scraps, particularly when I'm working on a project and need just a little bit of this or that or for sampler block quilts.

If you have a lot of scraps, consider putting some to good use by donating them to a quilt group that makes charity quilts, an animal shelter, or another worthy cause. One of my quilt guilds gives scraps to Habitat for Humanity, which shreds the fabric for insulation and other building materials. You may think that one day you will use it all, but chances are that you love fabric and will be bringing in new favorites to fill up your space. And keeping your quilting space clean and tidy helps open your mind to creativity.

I rarely keep scraps that are smaller than 1½″ in any dimension, even long strips. Skinny scraps are called *strings*; I don't normally keep these because it's unlikely that I'll make a project with one thin strip. However, if I have a particularly beautiful string, then I turn it into a rosette flower (see Rosette Flower, below).

Rosette Flower

Here's a quick tutorial on how to make these easy rosette flowers. All you need is a strip of fabric and hot glue.

Rosette flowers are an elegant way to make use of long, skinny scraps.

Back side of rosette

1. Start with a fabric strip about 1″ wide and 27″ long.

2. Make a knot at one end.

3. Hold the knot with the tail facing down.

4. Fold the fabric in half by its width and wrap it around the knot about 2 times. Hot glue it in place.

5. Twist and wrap around the center, hot gluing the wrapping together about every half-turn.

6. Continue twisting and wrapping around the center until there is about 2″ left in the fabric.

7. Fold the remaining fabric to the underside of your rosette and hot glue it in place.

Depending on how big you want your rosette, you can use longer or shorter, thinner or wider strips. Explore ideas on how to use these flowers—for example, as embellishments to a picture frame, headband, shirt, or wreath. You can embellish just about anything with these flowers.

STASH BUILDING

With your stash and scraps well sorted and stored, it's easy to see if you are missing certain colors or are too heavy on others. For example, I am a victim of small-scale prints and blue fabrics. Organization helps validate what you already know you love. It can also show you something you didn't know about yourself and equip you to be a better fabric shopper—one who fills in missing colors and types to grow a well-rounded stash.

Store scraps by color, but store stash fabric by both color and category.

Types of Fabric Prints

To build a diverse stash, start by assessing the kinds of fabrics you have. In addition to color, fabric can be categorized into four types of fabric prints:

- **Solids** are fabrics that are completely one color. These include fabrics that appear to have texture, such as solids with a linen or crosshatch look to them.

- **Geometric** fabrics feature designs that can be simple or complex, regimented or random, straight or curvy, or anywhere in between. They include polka dots, stripes, plaids, checks, and diamonds.

- **Floral** fabrics feature flowers. These are often feminine, pretty, and classic. Floral designs dominate over geometric design; a polka dot print with roses would be categorized as a floral print.

- **Novelty** fabrics are prints that encompass virtually everything else that doesn't fall in the solid, geometric, or floral prints categories. They feature motifs, such as trains, dogs, cherries, text, buildings, birds, or people. When there is a novety element, it sets the category. Specifically, a polka dot print with roses that includes bunnies would be considered a novelty print.

Fabric Shopping

Buying fabric is perhaps the best and most addictive part of quiltmaking. These days, there is such a wide and diverse range of fabrics that consistently beckons us to buy more. But wise choices make it easier to move our favorite fabrics from being stash to being design elements.

Smart buying is about knowing what you love, what you have, and what you don't have. Fill in gaps, but don't pass up the prints you love. Know that basics and solids will always be there, especially when you are shopping for a particular pattern. If you strategize, you will build a stash that is useful when it's time to put together a beautiful quilt.

Basics are the best kind of fabric prints to add to your stash. The fabrics are normally tone-on-tone or white-on-color fabric. These versatile prints can be pulled into virtually any color palette. They may be solids, textured solids, small scale, polka dots, stripes, text, or gingham.

I tend to buy fat quarter bundles of these basics and always have them replenished. If I'm buying off the bolts, I'll buy half-yard cuts for stash building. However, if I'm buying neutrals, I'll load up—usually anywhere from 2 to 6 yards—because I know that I use neutrals for many of my quilts.

Think twice before buying a lot of large-scale or multicolored prints, as they can be difficult to put into a quilt unless you are building the design around the fabric's palette. I buy them when I'm in love with the print; in that case, I'll buy anywhere from a half-yard to 6 yards. For borders and binding, 2 yards is a good amount. If I'm buying 6 yards, it's normally for the quilt back. If I'm in love with a large-print fabric, then it's because I love the color palette and will most likely build a future quilt around those colors.

TIP

Cotton Rule

Most quilters use 100% cotton fabric. Why cotton? It's easy to sew, feels soft, wears well, and isn't too stretchy. If you are going to choose a fabric other than 100% cotton, say a lovely cotton-linen blend, make sure the shrinkage is the same rate as the other fabrics in your project if you are not prewashing your fabric. Otherwise, choose not to wash your quilt.

SEWING NOTES

Here are some general sewing guidelines that apply to all quilt projects in this book:

- Yardage is based on 42″-wide cuts of fabric.

- All measurements include a ¼″ seam allowance, unless otherwise noted.

- Sew with right sides together.

- Arrows in diagrams show the direction for pressing seam allowances.

- All strips are measured selvage to selvage (width of fabric), unless otherwise noted.

- All binding measurements are based on 2½″-wide strips.

- Buy additional yardage for directional fabric.

- Test blocks are always a good idea, especially if you are a beginner.

Suggested fabric requirements can be used interchangeably with your scraps. When a pattern calls for fat quarters or yardages, you can pull from your scrap fabric to give your quilt a scrappier look. Pull enough scrap fabric to total the sum of the yardages required. Although cutting directions are given for cutting strips from the width of fabric, the number of units per shape size is also given.

puggles

Finished quilt: 48″ × 64″ • **Finished block:** 16″ × 16″

Pieced and machine quilted by Sandra Clemons

design thoughts

Color scheme: Harmonious, double complement: red-violet, yellow-green, blue-violet, and yellow-orange (see Harmonious Color Schemes, page 9).

Accent color: White—without the white to add lightness, this might have been a very somber quilt.

Design: I enjoy using nature as my muse to my quilt art. Denver's saturated blue skies and the lavender bushes throughout my yard inspired this quilt. Although I love the use of solids, sometimes I don't want the flat look that solids can give. I balance the solids by adding texture. Here I used a textured solid to give the quilt movement.

Hitting your stash and scraps: Don't have quite the yardage requirements for the quilt? Consider scrapping the background with a variety of fabrics that have the same value. If you want to change the colors for your quilt, try another harmonious color scheme. If you want a warmer look, try a warmer neutral for the background and a warm color, such as red, for the bold stars.

Fabric Requirements

Blue: 1½ yards or 8 fat quarters for background

Navy: ¾ yard or 4 fat quarters for squares and Flying Geese

White: ⅞ yard or 3 fat quarters for Flying Geese background

Scraps: ⅔ yard or 3 fat quarters for Flying Geese

Backing: 3 yards

Batting: 56″ × 72″

Binding: ½ yard

Cutting Instructions

BLUE

Cut 8 strips 6½″ × WOF.*

- Subcut into 48 squares 6½″ × 6½″.

NAVY

Cut 2 strips 4½″ × WOF.

- Subcut into 12 squares 4½″ × 4½″.

Cut 4 strips 2⅞″ × WOF.

- Subcut into 48 squares 2⅞″ × 2⅞″.
- Cut the squares diagonally once to make 96 half-square triangles.

WHITE

Cut 5 strips 5¼″ × WOF.

- Subcut into 36 squares 5¼″ × 5¼″.
- Cut the squares diagonally twice to make 144 quarter-square triangles.

SCRAPS

Cut 96 squares 2⅞″ × 2⅞″.

- Cut the squares diagonally once to make 192 half-square triangles.

BINDING

Cut 6 strips 2½″ × WOF.

* WOF = width of fabric

Block Construction

For some general sewing guidelines, refer to Sewing Notes (page 23). For detailed instructions on making Flying Geese, refer to Special Techniques (page 103).

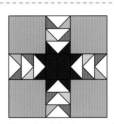

Puggles block assembly; make 12.

1. Sew together 2 small half-square triangles and 1 large white quarter-square triangle to make a Flying Geese unit. The corners of the small triangles will extend ¼″ beyond each end of the large triangle, creating an offset seam and dog-ears. Press seams toward the half-square triangles and trim the dog-ears. For each block, make 4 Flying Geese with navy fabric and 8 Flying Geese with scraps. **FIG. A**

2. Stitch together 3 Flying Geese. The navy geese should be at the bottom with 2 scrap Flying Geese units on top. Make 4. **FIG. B**

3. Stitch background squares to each side of the Flying Geese units made in Step 2. Make 2. **FIG. C**

A   B

C

4. Sew the remaining 2 Flying Geese units made in Step 2 to both sides of the navy square. **FIG. D**

D

5. Complete your block by stitching together the units from Steps 3 and 4. **FIG. E**

6. Repeat Steps 2–5 to make 12 blocks.

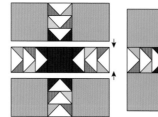
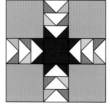

E

Assemble Quilt Top

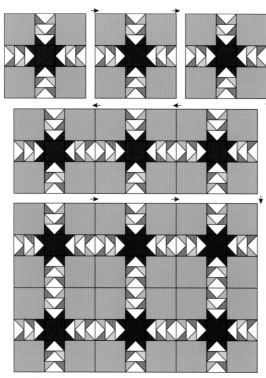

Puggles **quilt assembly**

1. Arrange the blocks as shown in the *Puggles* quilt assembly diagram.

2. Stitch together 3 blocks to make a row; press seams in one direction.

3. Stitch together the rows; press seams in one direction.

Finish Quilt

For instructions on quilt finishing, refer to Quiltmaking Basics (page 109).

1. Prepare and layer the quilt top, batting, and backing.

2. Quilt as desired.

3. Bind the quilt.

4. Add a label.

birds

Finished quilt: 72″ × 88″ • **Finished block:** 16″ × 16″

Pieced and machine quilted by Sandra Clemons

design thoughts

Color scheme: I started with a harmonious double complement of red and green, orange and navy blue, but I realized I liked it better without the green (see Harmonious Color Schemes, page 9).

Accent color: White—the white adds a lightness to the quilt and makes the colors pop.

Design: When selecting colors other than the neutrals, aim for an odd number of colors. Years back, my mother-in-law told me that in decorating, odd numbers create a more interesting look. The effect applies to quilting too. Along the same lines, vary the proportion of mixed colors and use brights sparingly for a bigger impact. In this quilt, I used three orange, two red, and two dark pink blocks as highlighting blocks. These pop against the navy blocks.

Hitting your stash and scraps: Instead of using one fabric for all four birds in the blocks, use a mix of scraps in similar colors to make each bird a bit different. Or try a different harmonious double-complement color scheme, such as soft colors in orange and blue, green and red with a warm background.

Fabric Requirements

Gray: 3 yards or 13 fat quarters for background

White: 2¾ yards or 22 fat quarters for birds

Fat quarters: 10 for birds (Each fat quarter makes 2 blocks; add more fabrics for more variety.)

Border: 1¼ yards

Backing: 5½ yards

Batting: 80″ × 96″

Binding: ⅔ yard

Cutting Instructions

GRAY

Cut 12 strips 5½″ × WOF.

- Subcut into 80 squares 5½″ × 5½″.
- Cut the squares diagonally once to make 160 half-square triangles.

Cut 9 strips 4¼″ × WOF.

- Subcut into 80 squares 4¼″ × 4¼″.
- Cut the squares diagonally once to make 160 half-square triangles.

WHITE

Cut 10 strips 2¾″ × WOF.

- Cut the strips in half across their width.

Cut 40 strips 1⅝″ × WOF.

- Cut the strips in half across their width.

FAT QUARTERS

Note: Cut your strips along the width of the fat quarter. For example, if the fat quarter measures 18″ × 22″, cut 18″ strips.

For each of the 10 fat quarters:

Cut 6 strips 1⅝″ × WOF.

Cut 4 strips 2¾″ × WOF.

BORDER

Cut 9 strips 4½″ × WOF.

- Stitch together the strips end to end.
- Subcut into 2 pieces 4½″ × 80½″ for side borders.
- Subcut into 2 pieces 4½″ × 72½″ for top and bottom borders.

BINDING

Cut 9 strips 2½″ × WOF.

ALTERNATIVE COLOR SCHEME

Change the look of your Birds quilt by altering the color scheme.

Block Construction

For some general sewing guidelines, refer to Sewing Notes (page 23). For detailed instructions on subcutting diamonds and pressing in a pinwheel, refer to Special Techniques (page 103).

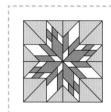

Birds block assembly; make 20.

1. Sew together a white strip 2¾˝ and a fat-quarter strip 1⅝˝ to make a Unit A strip. Make 4. **FIG. A**

2. From the Unit A strip, subcut 4 diamonds 2¾˝ wide at a 45° angle. Make 4. **FIG. B**

3. Sew together a white strip 1⅝˝ and a fat-quarter strip 2¾˝ to make a Unit B strip. **FIG. C**

4. From the Unit B strip, subcut 4 diamonds 1⅝˝ wide at a 45° angle. **FIG. D**

5. Stitch Unit A to Unit B. Make 4. **FIG. E**

6. Sew a white strip 1⅝˝ to each side of a fat-quarter strip 1⅝˝ to make a Unit C strip. **FIG. F**

7. From the Unit C strip, subcut 4 diamonds 1⅝˝ wide at a 45° angle. **FIG. G**

8. Sew a white strip 1⅝˝ to a fat-quarter strip 1⅝˝ to make a Unit D strip. **FIG. H**

9. From the Unit D strip, subcut 4 diamonds 1⅝˝ wide at a 45° angle, noting the direction of the cut. **FIG. I**

10. From the fat-quarter strip 2¾˝, subcut 4 diamonds 1⅝˝ wide at a 45° angle to make Unit E. **FIG. J**

11. Stitch Unit E to Unit D. Then stitch Unit C to Unit DE. **FIG. K**

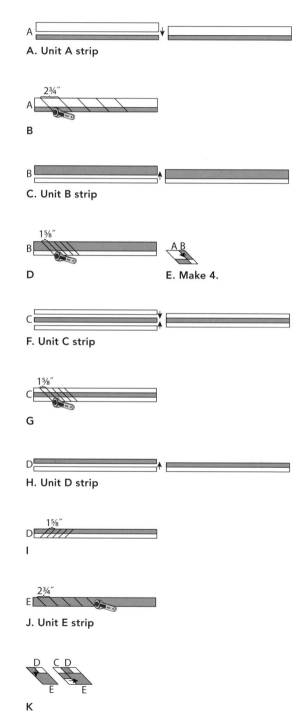

A. Unit A strip

C. Unit B strip

E. Make 4.

F. Unit C strip

H. Unit D strip

J. Unit E strip

12. Sew a large and a small gray half-square triangle to each side of an AB unit. Make 4. **FIG. L**

13. Sew a large and a small gray half-square triangle to each side of a CDE unit. Make 4. **FIG. M**

L. Make 4. M. Make 4.

14. Stitch together a unit from Step 12 and a unit from Step 13 to form a square. Make 4. **FIG. N**

15. Sew together 2 units from Step 14 to make the top half of the block. Make 2. **FIG. O**

N. Make 4. O. Make 2.

16. Sew together the units from Step 15. Press the seams in a pinwheel. **FIG. P**

17. Repeat Steps 1–16 to make 20 blocks.

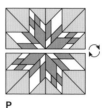

P

Assemble Quilt Top

Birds **quilt assembly**

1. Arrange the blocks as shown in the *Birds* quilt assembly diagram.

2. Stitch the blocks into rows. On the first, third, and fifth row, press the seams to the right. On the second and fourth rows, press the seams to the left.

3. Stitch together the rows and press the seams in one direction.

4. Attach the side borders first; then attach the top and bottom borders. Press the seams toward the borders.

Finish Quilt

For instructions on quilt finishing, refer to Quiltmaking Basics (page 109).

1. Prepare and layer the quilt top, batting, and backing.

2. Quilt as desired.

3. Bind the quilt.

4. Add a label.

twilight

Finished quilt: 84″ × 84″ • **Finished block:** 32″ × 32″

Pieced and machine quilted by Sandra Clemons

design thoughts

<u>Color scheme:</u> Calming, analogous, red-violet to violet to blue (see Calming Color Schemes, page 8).

<u>Accent colors:</u> Pink and lavender—the pinks and lavenders echo the darker colors of the stars and add depth and dimension.

<u>Design:</u> When making this quilt, I wanted to use dark purple and lavender to design a quilt that was a bit feminine, but mature and not girly. When selecting fabric from my stash, I needed more rich purples and lavender. At the time, the quilt market didn't have a lot of lavender—a reminder of why it's a good idea to maintain a well-rounded stash and to be patient. Sure enough, the next season included more lavender and purple fabrics.

<u>Hitting your stash and scraps:</u> Consider using low-volume scraps instead of a white background. Or perhaps, instead of using white in the pinwheels, use a medium-to-dark scrap for both the white and the color side of the half-square triangles within the pinwheels—just make sure there is enough contrast to see the design.

Fabric Requirements

White: 5¾ yards or 30 fat quarters

Light print scraps: ¾ yards or 3 fat quarters total

Dark print scraps: 1¼ yards or 5 fat quarters total

Navy: ¼ yard or 1 fat quarter

Backing: 6 yards

Batting: 94″ × 94″

Binding: ⅔ yard

Cutting Instructions

WHITE

Cut 8 strips 4½″ × WOF.

- Stitch together the strips end to end.
- Subcut into 2 pieces 4½″ × 76½″ for side borders.
- Subcut into 2 pieces 4½″ × 84½″ for top and bottom borders.

Cut 12 strips 2½″ × WOF.

- Stitch together the strips end to end.
- Subcut into 2 sashing strips 2½″ × 32½″.
- Subcut into 3 sashing strips 2½″ × 66½″.
- Subcut into 2 sashing strips 2½″ × 70½″.

Cut 4 strips 8½″ × WOF.

- Subcut into 16 squares 8½″ × 8½″.

Cut 2 strips 17¼″ × WOF.

- Subcut into 4 squares 17¼″ × 17¼″.
- Cut the squares diagonally twice to make 16 quarter-square triangles. Label these "A background triangles."

Cut 2 strips 8⅞″ × WOF.

- Subcut into 8 squares 8⅞″ × 8⅞″.
- Cut the squares diagonally once to make 16 half-square triangles. Label these "B background triangles."

Cut 11 strips 2⅞″ × WOF.

- Subcut into 144 squares 2⅞″ × 2⅞″.
- Cut the squares diagonally once to make 288 half-square triangles. Label these "C background triangles."

Cut 5 strips 3⅝″ × WOF for the pieced border.

- Subcut into 44 isosceles triangles using Pattern A (page 38).

Cut 4 squares 3⅞″ × 3⅞″ from the fabric left over from the previous cuts.

- Subcut the squares diagonally once to make 8 triangles for the pieced border.

LIGHT PRINT SCRAPS

Cut 80 squares 2⅞″ × 2⅞″.

- Cut the squares diagonally once to make 160 half-square triangles.

DARK PRINT SCRAPS

Cut 160 squares 2⅞″ × 2⅞″.

- Cut the squares diagonally once to make 320 half-square triangles.

NAVY

Cut 48 isosceles triangles from the remaining scraps of the dark print scraps using Pattern A (page 38).

Cut 4 squares 3½″ × 3½″.

BINDING

Cut 8 strips 2½″ × WOF.

Block Construction

For some general sewing guidelines, refer to Sewing Notes (page 23). For detailed instructions on making Flying Geese and pressing in a pinwheel, refer to Special Techniques (page 103).

Twilight block assembly; make 4.

1. Piece the light print scrap half-square triangles to the small background fabric half-square triangles to make triangle square units. Press the seams toward the colored fabrics. Make 24. **FIG. A**

2. Repeat with the dark print scrap triangles and the small background fabric triangles. Press the seams toward the colored fabrics. Make 48.

3. Arrange 6 light print triangle square units with 4 light half-square triangles to make a pieced triangle unit as shown. Sew together, pressing seams in alternate directions as shown. For 1 block you'll need 4 units made with light fabrics and 8 units made with dark fabrics. **FIG. B**

4. Make the center unit by stitching together a dark pieced triangle unit and a B background triangle. Make 4. Then, piece together those units to make a center unit. Press the seam in a pinwheel. **FIG. C**

5. Stitch together Flying Geese by sewing a light pieced triangle unit on the left, a dark pieced triangle unit on the right, and an A background triangle. The corners of the small triangles will extend ¼˝ beyond each end of the large triangle, creating an offset seam and dog-ears. Press seams toward the background fabric and trim the dog-ears. Repeat this step to make 4 Flying Geese. **FIG. D**

6. Add background squares to 2 of the Flying Geese units from Step 3. **FIG. E**

A

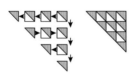

B. Pieced triangle unit

C. Center unit

D. Flying Geese

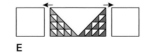
E

7. Sew the remaining 2 Flying Geese units to both sides of the center unit. **FIG. F**

8. Complete the block by stitching the rows together as shown in the block assembly diagram. **FIG. G**

9. Repeat Steps 1–8 to make 4 blocks.

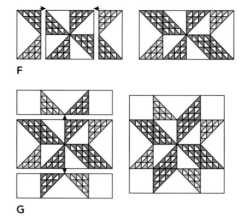

F

G

Assemble Border

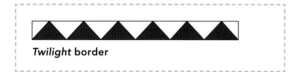

Twilight **border**

1. Sew together 12 dark isosceles triangles and 11 white isosceles triangles to make a border piece. Press seams toward the dark triangles (**FIG. H**). Make 4.

2. Stitch the white half-square triangles to both ends of each unit made in Step 1, offsetting seams and trimming dog-ears. **FIG. I**

3. Add the navy squares to both ends of 2 of the units made in Step 3 to make the top and bottom borders. (The remaining 2 border pieces are the side borders.) **FIG. J**

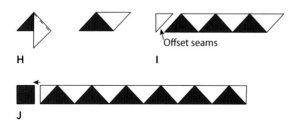

H   I

Offset seams

J

Assemble Quilt Top

Twilight **quilt assembly**

1. Arrange the sashings and blocks as shown in the *Twilight* quilt assembly diagram.

2. Stitch together the rows, pressing the seams toward the sashing units.

3. For the first border, stitch the side borders to the quilt top first, followed by the top and bottom borders. Press the seams toward the first border.

4. For the second border, stitch the side borders to the quilt top first, followed by the top and bottom borders. Press the seams toward the first border.

5. For the third border, stitch the side borders to the quilt top first, followed by the top and bottom borders. Press the seams toward the third border.

Finish Quilt

For instructions on quilt finishing, refer to Quiltmaking Basics (page 109).

1. Prepare and layer the quilt top, batting, and backing.

2. Quilt as desired.

3. Bind the quilt.

4. Add a label.

OPTION: twilight wallhanging

Finished quilt: 50″ × 50″
Finished block: 32″ × 32″

- -

For a smaller wallhanging version of Twilight, substitute the following fabric requirements and cutting instructions and refer to the Twilight wallhanging assembly diagram for placement. Follow all the construction and assembly directions for the main quilt, beginning at Block Construction (page 35).

Twilight wallhanging assembly

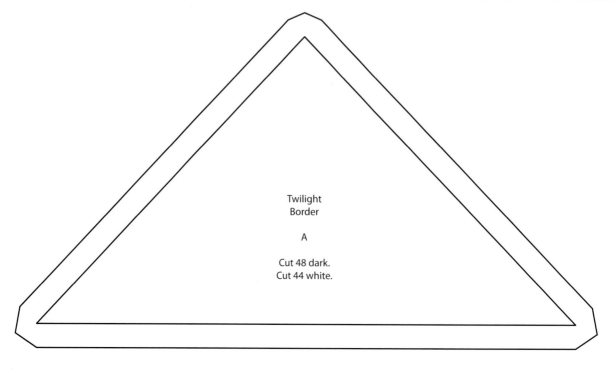

Twilight
Border

A

Cut 48 dark.
Cut 44 white.

Fabric Requirements

Background: 1½ yards or 6 fat quarters

Green: ½ yard or 2 fat quarters

Yellow: 1¼ yards or 5 fat quarters

Backing: 3 yards

Batting: 58″ × 58″

Binding: ½ yard

Cutting Instructions

BACKGROUND

Cut 1 strip 17¼″ × WOF.

- Subcut into 1 square 17¼″ × 17¼″.
- Cut the square diagonally twice to make 4 quarter-square triangles. Label these "A background triangles."
- Subcut into 4 squares 8½″ × 8½″.

Cut 1 strip 8⅞″ × WOF.

- Subcut into 2 squares 8⅞″ × 8⅞″.
- Cut the squares diagonally once to make 4 half-square triangles. Label these "B background triangles."

Cut 2 strips 2⅞″ × WOF.

- Subcut into 28 squares 2⅞″ × 2⅞″.
- Subcut the remaining pieces from previous cuts into 8 more squares 2⅞″ × 2⅞″.
- Cut all the squares diagonally once to make 72 half-square triangles. Label these "C background triangles."

Cut 4 strips 4½″ × WOF (for the first border).

- Stitch together the strips end to end.
- Subcut into 2 pieces 1½″ × 32½″ for side borders.
- Subcut into 2 pieces 1½″ × 40½″ for top and bottom borders.

GREEN

Cut 2 strips 2⅞″ × WOF.

- Subcut into 20 squares 2⅞″ × 2⅞″.
- Cut the squares diagonally once to make 40 half-square triangles.

Cut 5 strips 1½″ × WOF (for the second border).

- Subcut into 2 pieces 1½″ × 40½″ for side borders.
- Stitch together the remaining 3 strips end to end.
- Subcut into 2 pieces 1½″ × 42½″ for top and bottom borders.

YELLOW

Cut 6 strips 2⅞″ × WOF.

- Subcut into 40 squares 2⅞″ × 2⅞″.
- Cut the squares diagonally once to make 80 half-square triangles.

Cut 5 strips 4½″ × WOF (for the third border).

- Cut 2 pieces 4½″ × 42½″ for side borders.
- Stitch together the remaining 3 strips end to end.
- Subcut into 2 pieces 4½″ × 50½″ for top and bottom borders.

BINDING

Cut 6 strips 2½″ × WOF.

playful

Finished quilt: 64″ × 64″ • **Finished block:** 12″ × 12″

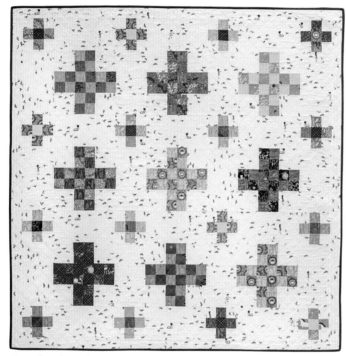

Pieced and machine quilted by Sandra Clemons

design thoughts

Color scheme: I used a focal fabric to pick out the specific colors for this quilt, but basically it includes variations of all the colors of the rainbow (see Rainbow Color Schemes, page 11).

Accent color: Yellow—the occasional squares of yellow add pops of brightness to this cheerful quilt.

Design: Playing at the park with my family inspired this quilt. My niece and nephew enjoy having me chase them around. The background print emphasizes this playfulness in both subject (children and flying birds) and design (the scattered motifs provide a light, airy feeling).

Hitting your stash and scraps: Add more scraps to the quilt by making all the pieces of the crosses from a mix of fabric. Or reverse the tone of the quilt by choosing a dark color for the background and light colors for the crosses.

Fabric Requirements

Background: 2¾ yards or 15 fat quarters

Scraps: 1⅓ yards total or 6 fat quarters

Backing: 4 yards

Batting: 62″ × 62″

Binding: ½ yard

Cutting Instructions

BACKGROUND

Cut 8 strips 6½″ × WOF.

- Subcut into 24 pieces 6½″ × 12½″ for sashing.

Cut 4 strips 4½″ × WOF.

- Subcut into 36 squares 4½″ × 4½″.

Cut 4 strips 2½″ × WOF.

- Subcut into 64 squares 2½″ × 2½″.

Cut 7 strips 2½″ × WOF for borders.

- Stitch together the strips end to end.
- Cut 2 strips 2½″ × 60½″ for side borders.
- Cut 2 strips 2½″ × 64½″ for top and bottom borders.

SCRAPS

Cut 260 squares 2½″ × 2½″.

BINDING

Cut 7 strips 2½″ × WOF.

Block Construction

For some general sewing guidelines, refer to Sewing Notes (page 23). For detailed instructions on pressing in a pinwheel, refer to Special Techniques (page 103).

BLOCK 1

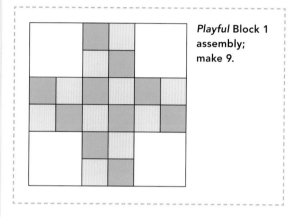

Playful Block 1 assembly; make 9.

1. Start by stitching the Four-Patch units. Mix and match 20 scrappy squares 2½″ × 2½″. For each of the 9 blocks, make 5 Four-Patch units. Press the seams in a pinwheel. **FIG. A**

2. Arrange the Four-Patches and the white background squares following the Block 1 assembly diagram. Sew the units into rows. Sew together the rows to make a Nine-Patch unit. Alternate pressing as shown. **FIG. B**

3. Repeat Steps 1 and 2 to make 9 blocks.

A. Make 5.

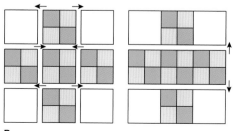

B

BLOCK 2

Playful Block 2 assembly; make 16.

1. Mix and match 5 dark squares for the cross and 4 background squares for the corners of the Nine-Patch. Arrange following the Block 2 assembly diagram. Sew together in rows. Alternate pressing as shown.

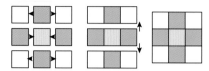

2. Repeat Step 1 to make 16 blocks.

Assemble Quilt Top

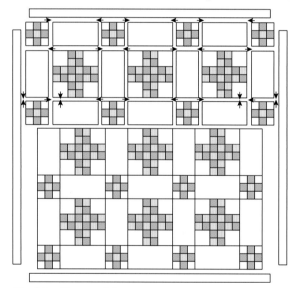

Playful quilt assembly

1. Arrange the blocks, Nine-Patches, and sashing as shown in the *Playful* quilt assembly diagram.

2. Stitch the units into rows, pressing seams toward the white sashing units.

3. Stitch together the rows and press the seams in one direction.

4. Attach the side borders first and then the top and bottom borders. Press the seams toward the borders.

Finish Quilt

For instructions on quilt finishing, refer to Quiltmaking Basics (page 109).

1. Prepare and layer the quilt top, batting, and backing.

2. Quilt as desired.

3. Bind the quilt.

4. Add a label.

Playful table runner assembly

OPTION: playful table runner

Finished runner: 28″ × 64″

For a table runner version of Playful, substitute the following fabric requirements and cutting instructions and refer to the Playful table runner assembly diagram for placement. Follow all the construction and assembly directions for the main quilt, beginning at Block Construction (page 41).

Fabric Requirements

Gray: 1½ yards or 8 fat quarters

Pink: ½ yard or 2 fat quarters

White: ¼ yard or 1 fat quarter

Backing: 2 yards

Batting: 36″ × 72″

Binding: ½ yard

Cutting Instructions

GRAY

Cut 4 strips 6½″ × WOF.

- Subcut into 10 pieces 6½″ × 12½″ for sashing.

Cut 2 strips 4½″ × WOF.

- Subcut into 12 squares 4½″ × 4½″.

Cut 2 strips 2½″ × WOF.

- Subcut into 32 squares 2½″ × 2½″.

Cut 5 strips 2½″ × WOF (for borders).

- Stitch together end to end.

- Subcut into 2 strips 2½″ × 60½″ for side borders.

- Subcut into 2 strips 2½″ × 28½″ for top and bottom borders.

PINK

Cut 5 strips 2½″ × WOF.

- Subcut into 70 squares 2½″ × 2½″.

WHITE

Cut 2 strips 2½″ × WOF.

- Subcut into 30 squares 2½″ × 2½″.

BINDING

Cut 5 strips 2½″ × WOF.

fiddlestars

Finished quilt: 80″ × 80″   •   **Finished block:** 24″ × 24″

design thoughts

Color scheme: Rainbow (see Rainbow Color Schemes, page 11).

Accent colors: Black and white—the black-and-white checkerboard adds a dynamic, high-contrast element to the design and balances the bright colors.

Pieced and machine quilted by Sandra Clemons

Design: What shapes do you see in this quilt? Yes, there are two. Either you see Sawtooth Stars or the Square-in-a-Square. I wanted to design a three-dimensional quilt. To add balance, I used black and white to articulate the design. I placed scrappy squares in a variety of colors but kept the scale relatively the same. The variety of scrappy colors compared with the neutrals provided enough contrast to add oomph to the quilt design.

Hitting your stash and scraps: For a quick switch, all the squares could be made from scrap fabrics. This design is really open to playing with color in interesting ways. Use scraps for the centers, make the points of the Sawtooth Stars with dark fabrics, and omit the chain by switching the background to low-volume colors.

Fabric Requirements

White: 1½ yards or 6 fat quarters (for Sawtooth Star points)

Black: 1¼ yards or 6 fat quarters (for chain)

Tan: 1½ yards or 7 fat quarters (for chain and Sawtooth Star center)

Fat quarters: 18 (for scrappy background fabric)

Backing: 5 yards

Batting: 88″ × 88″

Binding: ¾ yard

Cutting Instructions

WHITE

Cut 6 strips 6⅞″ × WOF.

- Subcut into 36 squares 6⅞″ × 6⅞″.
- Cut the squares diagonally once to make 72 half-square triangles.

BLACK

Cut 16 strips 2½″ × WOF.

- Subcut 1 strip into 16 squares 2½″ × 2½″.

TAN

Cut 20 strips 2½″ × WOF.

- Subcut 5 strips into 72 squares 2½″ × 2½″.

FAT QUARTERS

From *each* fat quarter:

Cut 1 strip 2⅞″ × WOF.

- Subcut into 6 squares 2⅞″ × 2⅞″.
- Cut the squares diagonally once to make 12 half-square triangles.

Cut 6 strips 2½″ × WOF.

- Subcut into 36 squares 2½″ × 2½″.

Note: After cutting all 18 fat quarters, you will have 216 half-square triangles and 648 squares 2½″ × 2½″.

BINDING

Cut 8 strips 2½″ × WOF.

Construction

For some general sewing guidelines, refer to Sewing Notes (page 23). For detailed instructions on pressing in a pinwheel, refer to Special Techniques (page 103).

STRIP PIECING

1. Stitch 2 black strips 2½″ × WOF to either side of a tan strip 2½″ × WOF, pressing the seams toward the black fabric. Make 5. **FIG. A**

2. Cut the 5 strip units made in Step 1 into 2½″-wide segments. Make 72. **FIG. B**

3. Stitch 2 tan strips 2½″ × WOF to either side of a black strip 2½″ × WOF, pressing the seams toward the black fabric. Make 5. **FIG. C**

4. Cut the 5 strip units made in Step 3 into 2½″-wide segments. Make 72. **FIG. D**

A

B

C

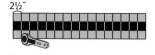

D

NINE-PATCH BLOCK

BLACK-AND-TAN NINE-PATCH BLOCKS

 Fiddlestars black-and-tan Nine-Patch block assembly; make 36.

Make a Nine-Patch block as shown in the black-and-tan assembly diagram, using the segments you made in Strip Piecing, Steps 1–4. You will use 2 black-tan-black segments and 1 tan-black-tan segment for each Nine-Patch block. Make 36.

SCRAPPY NINE-PATCH BLOCKS

For detailed instructions on locking seams and pressing in a pinwheel, refer to Special Techniques (page 103).

 Fiddlestars scrappy Nine-Patch block assembly; make 36.

1. Sew 2 fat-quarter squares 2½″ × 2½″ to either side of a tan square 2½″ × 2½″. Make 72 units. **FIG. E**

2. Sew together 2 units from Step 1 and a tan-black-tan unit made in Strip Piecing, Step 4, to make a scrappy Nine-Patch block. Make 36. **FIG. F**

3. Sew together 4 scrappy Nine-Patch blocks to make a Sawtooth Star center, locking the seams as you piece. Press the seams in a pinwheel. **FIG. G**

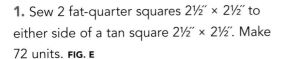

E

F

G

SAWTOOTH STAR

For detailed instructions on making Flying Geese, refer to Special Techniques (page 103).

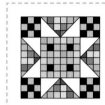

Fiddlestars **Sawtooth Star block assembly; make 9.**

1. Make Flying Geese blocks by first gathering your fat-quarter squares 2½″ × 2½″ and fat-quarter half-square triangles.

2. Sew together a pieced triangle using 3 of the squares and 3 of the half-square triangles as shown. Make 18 of each. **FIG. H & I**

3. Sew together a pieced triangle and a white half-square triangle. **FIG. J**

4. Sew together 2 units from Step 3 to make a Flying Geese unit. Make 36. **FIG. K**

5. Piece together a Sawtooth Star block as shown in the assembly diagram. **FIG. L**

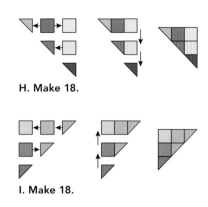

H. Make 18.

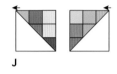

I. Make 18.

J

K

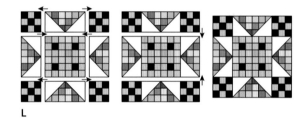

L

Assemble Quilt Top

Fiddlestars **quilt assembly**

Finish Quilt

For instructions on quilt finishing, refer to Quiltmaking Basics (page 109).

1. Prepare and layer the quilt top, batting, and backing.

2. Quilt as desired.

3. Bind the quilt.

4. Add a label.

1. Make sashing strips by sewing together 12 squares as shown. Make 24. Do not press the seams yet.

2. Arrange Sawtooth Star blocks and the remaining black and fat-quarter squares as shown in the *Fiddlestars* quilt top assembly diagram.

3. Stitch together the quilt top by working row by row. The sashing seams will fold right or left, depending on the direction of the adjacent seams on the Sawtooth Star blocks. Finger-press the sashing seams first and then finish off with an iron.

bracelet

Finished quilt: 76″ × 90″   •   **Finished block:** 12″ × 12″

Pieced and machine quilted by Sandra Clemons

design thoughts

Color scheme: I used a focal fabric to pick out the specific colors for this quilt, but basically it includes variations of a harmonious, double-complementary color scheme: blues and oranges, red-violets, and yellow-greens (see Harmonious Color Schemes, page 9).

Accent color: Dark pink—the dark pink squares add an element of rhythm to the quilt and provide a counterpoint to the stars.

Design: The stars seem to float on top of this quilt. The illusion that the stars are twinkling is created by having the solids and prints paired with a large, flat gray background.

Hitting your stash and scraps: Do you like your borders to stand out? I wanted the stars to float on top of the whole quilt, but you could frame the stars by using border fabric that contrasts with the background fabric. Use various backgrounds with a similar value for a scrappier look.

Fabric Requirements

Gray: 5½ yards or 24 fat quarters

Pink: ¼ yard or 1 fat quarter

Fat quarters: 12 (for blocks)

Backing: 6 yards

Batting: 84″ × 98″

Binding: ¾ yard

Cutting Instructions

For instructions on cutting triangles from strips, refer to Special Techniques (page 103).

GRAY

Cut 9 strips 4½″ × WOF (for the border).

- Stitch the strips end to end.
- Subcut into 2 strips 4½″ × 82½″ for side borders.
- Subcut into 2 strips 4½″ × 76½″ for top and bottom borders.

Cut 17 strips 2½″ × WOF.

- Subcut into 49 pieces 2½″ × 12½″.

Cut 14 strips 4½″ × WOF.

- Subcut into 120 squares 4½″ × 4½″.

Cut 8 strips 5⅜″ × WOF.

- Subcut into 120 rectangles 5⅜″ × 2⅝″.
- Cut 60 rectangles diagonally once to make long triangles. Note the direction of the cut.

- Cut the remaining 30 rectangles diagonally once in the opposite direction to make long triangles.

PINK

Cut 2 strips 2½″ × WOF.

- Subcut into 20 squares 2½″ × 2½″.

FAT QUARTERS

From *each* fat quarter:

Cut 1 strip 5¼″ × WOF.

- Subcut into 3 squares 5¼″ × 5¼″.
- Cut the squares diagonally twice to make 12 quarter-square triangles

Cut 2 strips 4⅞″ × WOF.

- Subcut into 10 isosceles triangles using Pattern A (page 56).

BINDING

Cut 9 strips 2½″ × WOF.

Block Construction

For some general sewing guidelines, refer to Sewing Notes (page 23). For detailed instructions on pressing in a pinwheel, refer to Special Techniques (page 103).

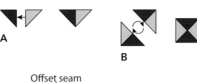

A

B

Offset seam

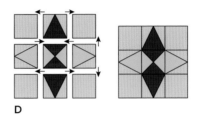

C

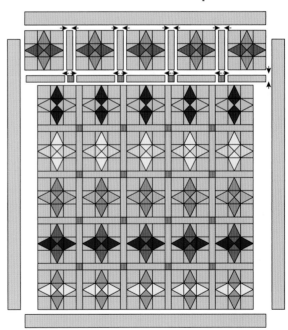

D

Bracelet **block assembly; make 30.**

1. Select pieces cut from 2 fat-quarter fabrics and gray background and arrange them as shown in the block assembly diagram.

2. Stitch together 2 quarter-square triangles of each fat-quarter fabric for the block's center unit. Make 2 units. Press the seams to the left. **FIG. A**

3. Stitch together the 2 units from Step 2 to make an hourglass unit. Press the seam in a pinwheel. **FIG. B**

4. Make 4 rectangle triangle units by stitching long triangles to each side of an isosceles triangle. The corners of the long triangles will extend ¼˝ beyond each end of the isosceles triangle, creating an offset seam and dog-ears. Press seams toward the long triangles and trim the dog-ears. This unit measures 4½˝ × 4½˝. Make 2 from each fat quarter. **FIG. C**

5. Complete your block by stitching together the units. **FIG. D**

6. Repeat Steps 1–5 to make 30 blocks.

Assemble Quilt Top

Bracelet quilt assembly

1. Arrange the sashing, pink square cornerstones, and blocks as shown in the *Bracelet* quilt assembly diagram.

2. Stitch together the sashing pieces and blocks to form rows, pressing the seams toward the sashing. Stich together the sashing pieces and cornerstones to form rows, pressing the seams toward the sashing.

3. Stitch together the rows to make the quilt center, pressing the seams toward the sashing rows.

4. Attach the side borders and then attach the top and bottom borders. Press the seams toward the borders.

Finish Quilt

For instructions on quilt finishing, refer to Quiltmaking Basics (page 109).

1. Prepare and layer the quilt top, batting, and backing.

2. Quilt as desired.

3. Bind the quilt.

4. Add a label.

OPTION: alternative bracelet quilt top

Alternative *Bracelet* quilt top

Finished quilt: 48″ × 64″
Finished block: 12″ × 12″

Give Bracelet a whole new look and a lot of drama by using just five pieced blocks in a column.

Fabric Requirements

Background: 2½ yards
(This design doesn't lend itself to fat quarters for the background.)

Fat quarters: 2

Backing: 3½ yards

Batting: 56″ × 72″

Binding: ½ yard

Cutting Instructions

For instructions on cutting triangles from strips, refer to Special Techniques (page 103).

BACKGROUND

Cut a strip 60½″ × *length* of fabric.

- Subcut into 1 unit 12½″ × 60½″.
- Subcut into 1 unit 24½″ × 60½″.
- Subcut into 2 units 2½″ × 48½″.

Cut 3 strips 4½″ × WOF.

- Subcut into 20 squares 4½″ × 4½″.

Cut 2 strips 5⅜″ × WOF.

- Subcut into 20 rectangles 5⅜″ × 2⅝″.
- Cut 10 rectangles diagonally once to make long triangles. Note the direction of the cut.

- Cut the remaining 10 rectangles diagonally once in the opposite direction to make long triangles.

FAT QUARTERS

From *each* fat quarter:

Cut 1 strip 5¼″ × 18″.

- Subcut into 3 squares 5¼″ × 5¼″.
- Cut the squares diagonally twice to make 12 quarter-square triangles. *Note: You will have 2 extra triangles.*

Cut 2 strips 4¼″ × 18″.

- Subcut into 10 isosceles triangles using Pattern A (below).

BINDING

Cut 6 strips 2½″ × WOF.

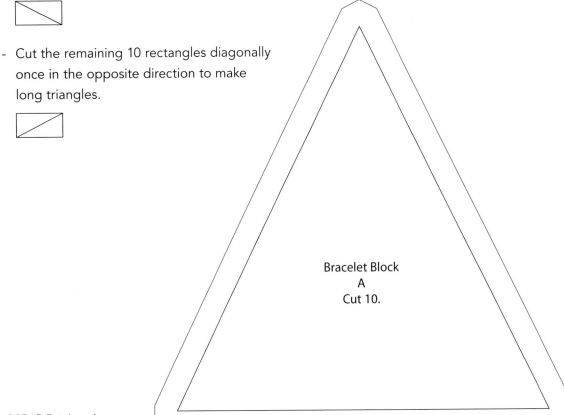

Bracelet Block
A
Cut 10.

meadows

Finished quilt: 64″ × 64″ • **Finished block:** 16″ × 16″

design thoughts

Color scheme: This quilt uses two sets of analogous colors—green and blue-green, orange and yellow-orange—in a way that is almost a split complementary. The result is a harmonious color scheme with pops of color to add vibrancy (see Color Relationships, page 7).

Pieced and machine quilted by Sandra Clemons

Accent color: Dark teal—the pops of teal add movement and interest.

Design: The block is a traditional design with the look of diamonds, but it is easy to make using half-square triangles instead. The random placement of the darker-value triangles adds depth and movement to each block.

Hitting your stash and scraps: Pick a different pair of analogous colors for a different look. Add more contrast to the quilt by using dark fabrics for the exploding stars and low-volume fabric for the block background and sashing.

Fabric Requirements

Substitute scrap fabric for the fat quarters if you like. You'll need enough to cut 320 squares 2⅞″ × 2⅞″.

Green: 1¾ yards for the sashing and borders

Background: 1½ yards or 8 fat quarters

Fat quarters: 8 (or more for a scrappier look)

Backing: 4 yards

Batting: 72″ × 72″

Binding: ½ yard

Cutting Instructions

GREEN

Cut 3 strips 16½″ × WOF.

- Subcut into segments 4½″ wide to make 24 sashing pieces.

BACKGROUND

Cut 5 strips 2½″ × WOF.

- Subcut into 72 squares 2½″ × 2½″.

Cut 4 strips 2½″ × WOF.

- Subcut into 36 rectangles 2½″ × 4½″.

Cut 3 strips 5¼″ × WOF.

- Subcut into 18 squares 5¼″ × 5¼″.

- Cut the squares diagonally twice to make 72 quarter-square triangles.

Cut 4 strips 3¼″ × WOF.

- Subcut into 52 squares 3¼″ × 3¼″.

FAT QUARTERS OR SCRAPS

Cut 320 squares 2⅞″ × 2⅞″.

- Cut the squares diagonally once to make 640 half-square triangles (64 triangles for sashing blocks and 576 triangles for big blocks).

BINDING

Cut 7 strips 2½″ × WOF.

Block Construction

For some general sewing guidelines, refer to Sewing Notes (page 23). For detailed instructions on making Flying Geese and Square-in-a-Square units and pressing in a pinwheel, refer to Special Techniques (page 103).

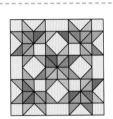

Meadows block assembly; make 9.

1. Sew 2 fat quarter half-square triangles to a background quarter-square triangle to make a Flying Geese unit. The corners of the small triangles will extend ¼″ beyond each end of the large triangle, creating an offset seam and dog-ears. Press seams toward the half-square triangles and trim the dog-ears. Make 8 for each block.

FIG. A

A

2. Sew 2 fat quarter half-square triangles to opposite sides of a background 3¼″ × 3¼″ square. Press away from the background fabric. Sew 2 fat quarter half-square triangles to the other sides of the square. Press away from the background fabric. Repeat to make 4 Square-in-a-Square units for each block. **FIG. B**

B

3. Sew together 2 half-square triangles to make a triangle square unit. Repeat to make 16 triangle square units for each block. Press the seams to one side. **FIG. C**

C

4. Stitch together 2 units from Step 3 as shown. Lock the seams. Make 6 for each block. **FIG. D**

D

5. Stitch 1 unit from Step 3 to a 2½″ background square. Press toward the triangle square unit. Make 4. **FIG. E**

E

6. Stitch together 2 units from Step 4. Press the seam in a pinweel. Make 1. **FIG. F**

F

7. Stitch a unit from Step 4 to a unit from Step 5. Press the seam in a pinwheel. Make 4. **FIG. G**

G

8. Stitch together the block with units made in Steps 1, 2, 6, and 7, while adding 4 background rectangles and 4 background squares. Alternate pressing as shown. **FIG. H**

9. Repeat Steps 1–8 to make 9 blocks.

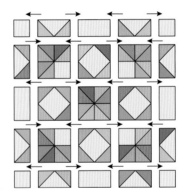

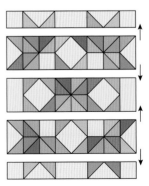

H

Cornerstone Construction

For detailed instructions on making Square-in-a-Square units, refer to Special Techniques (page 103).

 Meadows **cornerstone assembly; make 16.**

Sew 2 fat quarter half-square triangles to opposite sides of a background 3¼″ × 3¼″ square. Press away from the white fabric. Sew 2 fat quarter half-square triangles to the other sides of the square. Press away from the white fabric. Repeat to make 16 pieced cornerstones.

Assemble Quilt Top

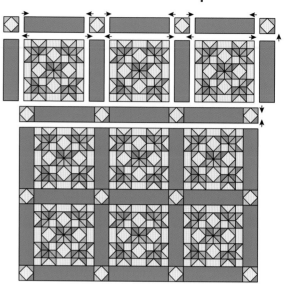

Meadows **quilt assembly**

1. Arrange the quilt top as shown in the *Meadows* quilt assembly diagram.

2. Stitch together cornerstone squares and sashing pieces to form rows, pressing the seams toward the sashing. Attach sashing pieces to the blocks, forming rows and pressing the seams toward the sashing.

3. Sew together the rows and press the seams in one direction.

Finish Quilt

For instructions on quilt finishing, refer to Quiltmaking Basics (page 109).

1. Prepare and layer the quilt top, batting, and backing.

2. Quilt as desired.

3. Bind the quilt.

4. Add a label.

delightful

Finished quilt: 64″ × 64″ • **Finished block:** 16″ × 16″

design thoughts

Color scheme: Rainbow, using tints, tones, and shades of all the colors (see Rainbow Color Schemes, page 11).

Accent color: Blue—the dark navy blue provides high contrast to the bright colors and the white background.

Design: This is a high-contrast, vibrant design. Solids can make a quilt feel flat and dull, but here's an exception. Beautiful and full of movement, the Carpenter's Wheel blocks give this quilt the feeling of rotation because of the accent pinwheels. In addition, the arrows in the borders give the quilt some spin. The use of values from light to dark in the blocks also adds movement, as some pieces stand out while others blend into the background.

Hitting your stash and scraps: For this quilt I added a design element by organizing color throughout the quilt. For example, I made sure that the center pinwheels were made of the same fabric within each block—you may not want to do this. You could randomly place color throughout the entire quilt. When I make another one, I will play with warm and cool tones. It would be so much fun to make every other block in cool scrappy fabrics and the others in warm colors. Or try a totally different look by swapping out the darks and lights.

Pieced and machine quilted by Sandra Clemons

Fabric Requirements

White: 2⅔ yards or 14 fat quarters

Scrap fabric: total of 2½ yards, or 13 fat quarters

Backing: 4 yards

Batting: 72″ × 72″

Binding: ½ yard

Cutting Instructions

WHITE

Cut 3 strips 2½″ × WOF.

- Subcut into 6 sashing units 2½″ × 16½″.

Cut 9 strips 2½″ × WOF.

- Stitch together the strips end to end.
- Subcut into 4 sashing units 2½″ × 52½″.
- Subcut into 2 sashing units 2½″ × 56½″.

Cut 9 strips 2½″ × WOF.

- Subcut into 72 squares 2½″ × 2½″.
- Subcut into 36 rectangles 2½″ × 4½″.

Cut 4 strips 5¼″ × WOF.

- Subcut into 32 squares 5¼″ × 5¼″.
- Cut each square diagonally twice to make 128 quarter-square triangles (72 for blocks and 56 for borders). Label these "A background triangles."

Cut 3 strips 3¼″ × WOF.

- Subcut into 36 squares 3¼″ × 3¼″.

Use the leftover pieces to cut 4 squares 4½″ × 4½″.

SCRAPS

Cut 344 squares 2⅞″ × 2⅞″.

- Cut the squares diagonally once to make 688 half-square triangles for blocks (112 half-square triangles are used for the border). Label these "B fat-quarter triangles."

Cut 14 squares 5¼″ × 5¼″.

- Cut the squares diagonally twice to make 56 quarter-square triangles. Label these "A fat-quarter triangles."

BINDING

Cut 7 strips 2½″ × WOF.

Block Construction

For some general sewing guidelines, refer to Sewing Notes (page 23). For detailed instructions on making Flying Geese and Square-in-a-Square units and pressing in a pinwheel, refer to Special Techniques (page 103).

A. Make 4.   **Make 4.**

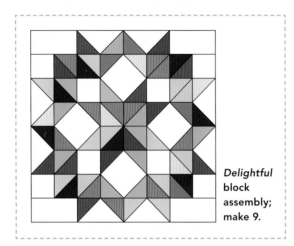

Delightful block assembly; make 9.

B

C

D

E

F

G

H

1. Sew 2 B fat-quarter triangles to an A background triangle to make a Flying Geese unit. The corners of the small triangles will extend ¼″ beyond each end of the large triangle, creating an offset seam and dog-ears. Press the seams as shown and trim the dog-ears. Make 8 for each block. **FIG. A**

2. Sew together 2 B fat-quarter half-square triangles to make a triangle square unit. Repeat to make 16 triangle square units for each block. Press the seams as desired. **FIG. B**

3. Sew together 2 units from Step 2. Make 2. **FIG. C**

4. Sew together 2 units from Step 3 for the block center. Press the seam in a pinwheel. **FIG. D**

5. Sew together 2 units from Step 2. Make 4. **FIG. E**

6. Sew a unit from Step 2 to a 2½″ background square. Press the seam to the triangle square unit. Make 4. **FIG. F**

7. Sew together a unit from Step 5 and a unit from Step 6. Make 4. Press the seam in a pinwheel. **FIG. G**

8. Sew 2 B fat-quarter triangles to opposite sides of a background 3¼″ × 3¼″ square. Press away from the white fabric. Sew 2 B fat-quarter triangles to the other sides of the square. Press away from the white fabric. Repeat to make 4 Square-in-a-Square units. **FIG. H**

9. Sew 2 units from Step 7 to either side of a unit from Step 8, paying careful attention to the direction of the Step 6 units. Make 2. **FIG. I**

10. Sew 2 units from Step 8 to either side of the unit from Step 7. Make 1. **FIG. J**

11. Sew 2 Flying Geese from Step 1 to 2 background squares. Make 2. **FIG. K**

12. Sew 2 Flying Geese from Step 1 to 2 background rectangles. Make 2. **FIG. L**

13. Sew together the rows, pressing the seams as shown. **FIG. M**

14. Repeat Steps 1–13 to make 9 blocks.

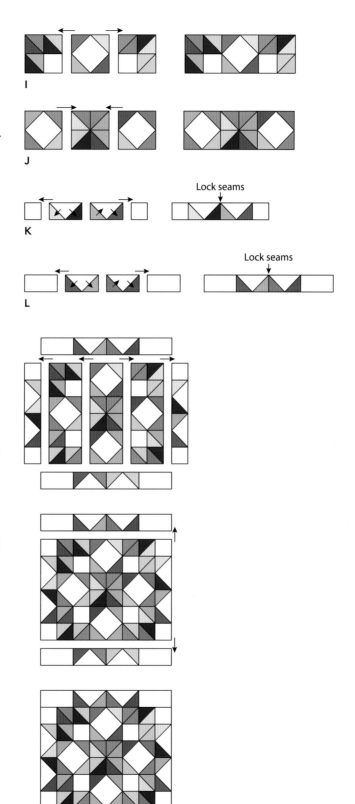

I

J

Lock seams

K

Lock seams

L

M

Assemble Pieced Border

N

1. Make 112 Flying Geese. Make 56 with an A background triangle and 56 with an A fat-quarter triangle. **FIG. N**

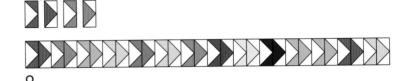

O

2. Sew together 28 Flying Geese units for each border as shown. Make 4. **FIG. O**

P

3. Add the background cornerstone to 2 border units from Step 2. **FIG. P**

Assemble Quilt Top

Delightful quilt assembly

1. Arrange the blocks, sashing units, and borders as shown in the *Delightful* quilt assembly diagram.

2. Stitch together blocks and sashing units to form rows, pressing seam allowances toward the sashing.

3. Stitch the rows together, pressing seam allowances toward the sashing.

4. Add the first border by stitching the sides first and then the top and bottom.

5. Attach the pieced side borders first and then the top and bottom borders. Press the seam allowances toward the borders.

Finish Quilt

For instructions on quilt finishing, refer to Quiltmaking Basics (page 109).

1. Prepare and layer the quilt top, batting, and backing.

2. Quilt as desired.

3. Bind the quilt.

4. Add a label.

watermelon

Finished quilt: 56″ × 56″

Finished blocks: Medallion block: 17″ × 17″ • Jewel block: 6″ × 6″
25-Patch block: 6″ × 6″ • Triangle Patch block: 12″ × 12″

design thoughts

<u>Color scheme:</u> This quilt doesn't fit into any of the "official" color schemes. I selected the fabrics and colors because I liked the way they looked together—a good lesson in following your instincts when it comes to picking fabrics.

<u>Accent color:</u> Yellow—the pop of yellow brings your eye right to the quilt's center.

<u>Design:</u> The classic Churn Dash block was my inspiration for this quilt. You can see it as the framework for this design if you look at the blocks with the red background fabrics. I used the bold setting to place the many patterns within it. The high-contrast Jewel blocks grab your attention, while the low-volume 25-Patch blocks add subtle texture.

Pieced and machine quilted by Sandra Clemons

<u>Hitting your stash and scraps:</u> Reverse the tones of the Churn Dash blocks. Use a dark color in place of the whites and low-volume hues, and use lights and mediums for the Triangle Patch and Jewel blocks.

Fabric Requirements

White: 2 yards or 8 fat quarters

Backing: 3½ yards

Batting: 64″ × 64″

Binding: ½ yard

MEDALLION BLOCK:

Red, pink, light blue, and navy:
fat eighth of each

Yellow and green: fat quarter of each

JEWEL BLOCK:

Light blue, green, pink, and red:
fat quarter of each

Navy: half yard or 2 fat quarters

25-PATCH BLOCK:

Low-volume scraps: 1 yard total
or 4 fat quarters

TRIANGLE PATCH BLOCK:

Pink: fat eighth

Red: fat quarter

Cutting Instructions

For instructions on how to cut out pattern shapes from fabric strips, refer to Special Techniques (page 103).

WHITE
Cut 2 strips 12⅞″ × WOF.

- Subcut into 4 squares 12⅞″ × 12⅞″.
- Cut diagonally once to make 8 half-square triangles.

Cut 6 strips 4½″ × WOF (for border).

- Stitch together the strips end to end.
- Subcut into 2 side borders 4½″ × 48½″.
- Subcut into 2 top and bottom borders 4½″ × 56½″.

MEDALLION BLOCK FABRICS

To cut pieces for the Medallion block, use Patterns A–J (pages 76–78).

Red

Cut 4 of Pattern A from strips 2⅛″ wide.

Pink

Cut 4 of Pattern B from strips 2⅛″ wide.

Light blue

Cut 4 of Pattern C from strips 2 ¼″ wide.

Navy

Cut 4 of Pattern D from strips 2 ¼″ wide.

Yellow

Cut 4 each of Patterns E, F, G, and H from strips 2⅜″ wide (16 pieces total).

Green

Cut 4 each of Patterns I and J from strips 4⅛″ wide (8 pieces total).

JEWEL BLOCK FABRICS

To cut pieces for the Jewel block, use Patterns A, B, and C (page 78).

Light blue

Cut 64 isosceles triangles of Pattern A from strips 1⅝″ wide.

Continued on page 70

Continued from page 69

Green

Cut 64 isosceles triangles of Pattern B from strips 1⅝″ wide.

Pink

Cut 36 isosceles triangles of Pattern A and 36 isosceles triangles of Pattern B from strips 1⅝″ wide.

Red

Cut 36 isosceles triangles of Pattern A and 36 isosceles triangles of Pattern B from strips 1⅝″ wide.

Navy

Cut 128 isosceles triangles of Pattern C from 4 strips 2⅝″ wide.

25-PATCH BLOCK

Scraps

Cut 400 squares 1¾″ × 1¾″.

TRIANGLE PATCH BLOCK

Pink

Cut 6 squares 4⅞″ × 4⅞″.
- Cut diagonally once to make 12 half-square triangles.

Red

Cut 12 squares 4⅞″ × 4⅞″.
- Cut diagonally once to make 24 half-square triangles.

BINDING

Cut 6 strips 2½″ × WOF.

Medallion Block Construction

For some general sewing guidelines, refer to Sewing Notes (page 23). For instructions on making a Y-seam and pressing in a pinwheel, refer to Special Techniques (page 103).

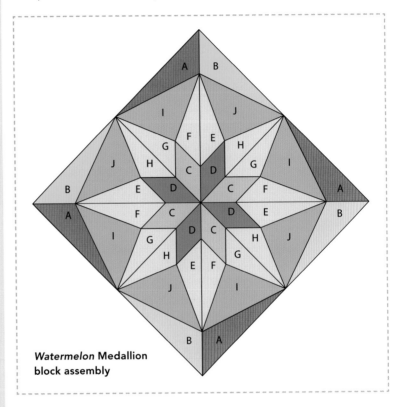

Watermelon **Medallion block assembly**

1. Gather pieces D, E, H, J, and A before stitching. **FIG. A**

2. Sew together the light blue diamond D and the yellow fabric E to make a DE unit. **FIG. B**

3. Sew together a yellow fabric H and a green fabric J to make an HJ unit. **FIG. C**

4. Sew together the DE and HJ units with a Y-seam. **FIG. D**

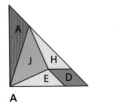

A

B. CE unit

C. HJ unit

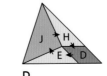

D

5. Sew together the unit from Step 4 and a red fabric A. The corner of the small triangle will extend ¼″ beyond the end of the large triangle, creating an offset seam and a dog-ear. Trim the dog-ear. **FIG. E**

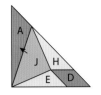

E

6. Gather pieces C, F, G, J, and B before stitching. Repeat Steps 1–5 with the mirror-image units. **FIG. F**

7. Repeat Steps 1–6 to make 4 units of each color combination.

8. Sew together 8 units as shown in the Medallion block assembly diagram. The block finishes at 17″ × 17″.

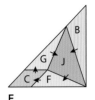

F

Jewel Block Construction

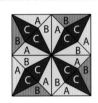

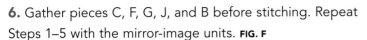

Watermelon Jewel block assembly; make 16.

1. Sew a pink A triangle to the right side of a navy C triangle. Sew a red B triangle to the left side of the navy C triangle. Make 4. **FIG. G**

2. Sew a light blue B triangle to the right side of a navy C triangle. Sew a light green A triangle to the left side of the navy C triangle. Make 4. **FIG. H**

3. Sew together a unit from Step 1 and a unit from Step 2. Repeat to make 4. Press 2 to one side and the other 2 to the other side. **FIG. I**

4. Sew together the combined units from Step 3. Make 2. **FIG. J**

5. Sew together the units from Step 4. Press the seam in a pinwheel. **FIG. K**

6. Repeat Steps 1–4 to make 16 blocks.

G

H

I. Make 2.   Make 2.

J

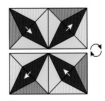

K

25-Patch Block Construction

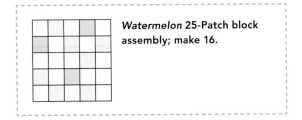

Watermelon 25-Patch block assembly; make 16.

Arrange 25 scrap squares as shown in the *Watermelon* 25-Patch block assembly diagram and sew them together to make a block. Make 16. The block finishes at 6″ × 6″.

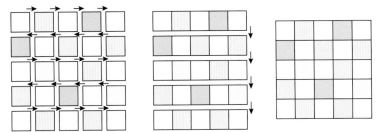

Press seams in direction of arrows.

Triangle Patch Block Construction

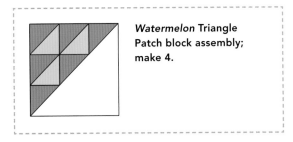

Watermelon Triangle Patch block assembly; make 4.

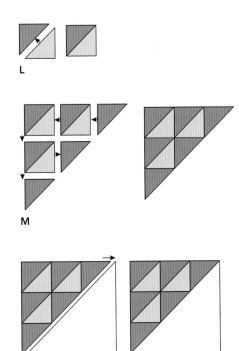

L

M

N

1. Sew 3 red and 3 pink half-square triangles together to make 3 triangle square units per block. Press seam allowances toward the red fabric. **FIG. L**

2. Sew the triangle square units into rows with 3 red half-square triangles. Sew the rows together. **FIG. M**

3. Add a large white half-square triangle to the unit from Step 2. Press the seam toward the white fabric. **FIG. N**

4. Repeat Steps 1–3 to make 4 blocks. The block finishes at 12″ × 12″.

Assemble Quilt Top

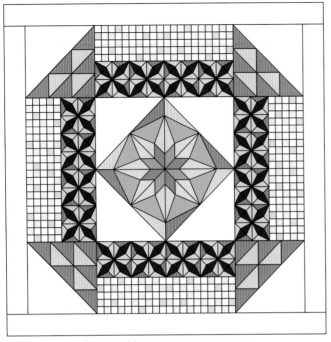

Watermelon **quilt assembly**

1. Sew a white half-square triangle to each side of the Medallion block. Press seams toward the white triangles. **FIG. O**

2. Sew together four 25-Patch and Jewel blocks. Press seams in the direction of the arrows. Make 4. **FIG. P**

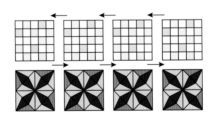

O

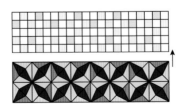

P

3. Sew 2 units from Step 2 to either side of the Medallion block. **FIG. Q**

4. Sew 2 Triangle Patch blocks to both sides of a remaining unit from Step 2. Make 2. **FIG. R**

5. Stitch together the quilt top. **FIG. S**

6. Attach the side borders first and then the top and bottom borders. Press the seams toward the borders.

Finish Quilt

For instructions on quilt finishing, refer to Quiltmaking Basics (page 109).

1. Prepare and layer the quilt top, batting, and backing.

2. Quilt as desired.

3. Bind the quilt.

4. Add a label.

Q

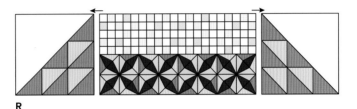

R

S

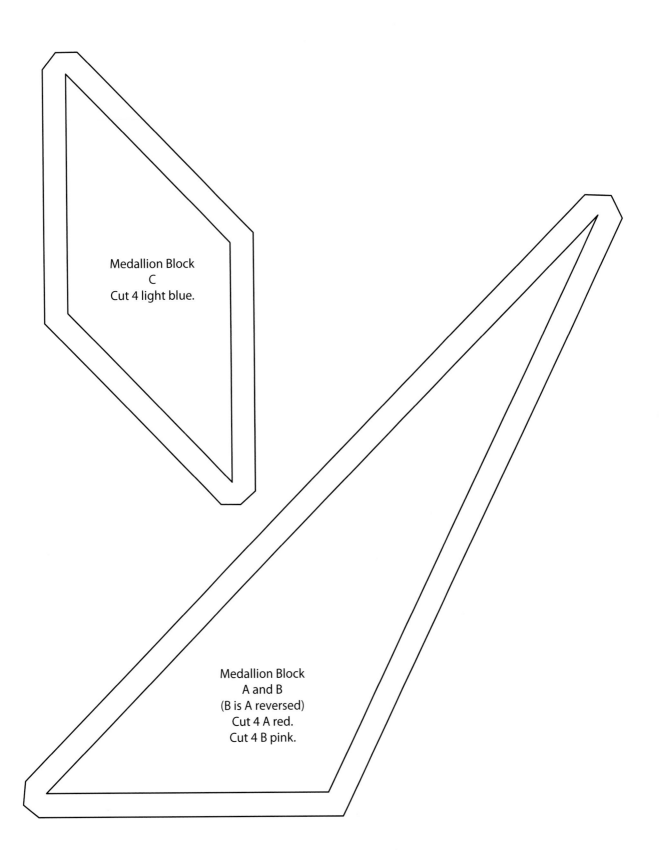

Medallion Block
C
Cut 4 light blue.

Medallion Block
A and B
(B is A reversed)
Cut 4 A red.
Cut 4 B pink.

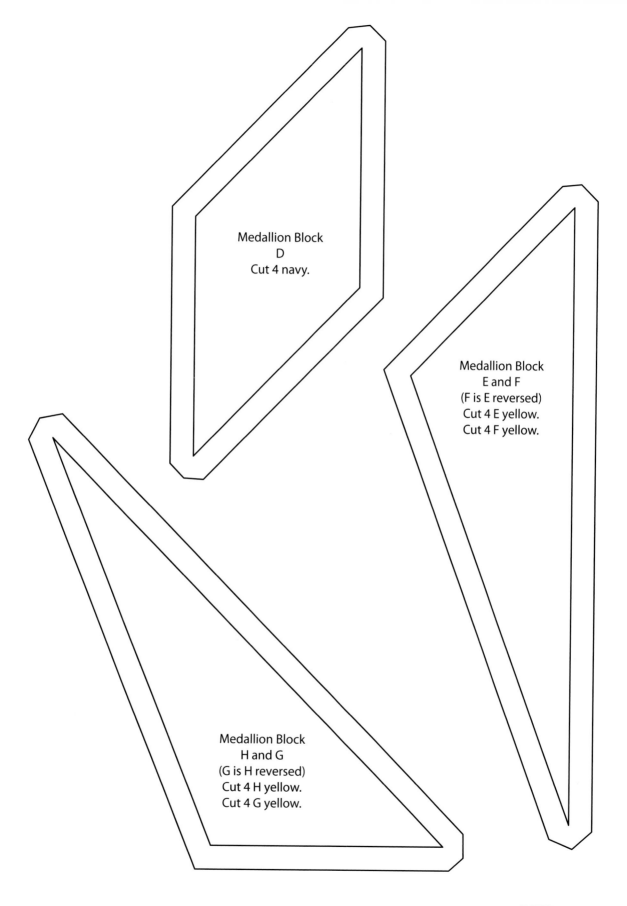

Medallion Block
D
Cut 4 navy.

Medallion Block
E and F
(F is E reversed)
Cut 4 E yellow.
Cut 4 F yellow.

Medallion Block
H and G
(G is H reversed)
Cut 4 H yellow.
Cut 4 G yellow.

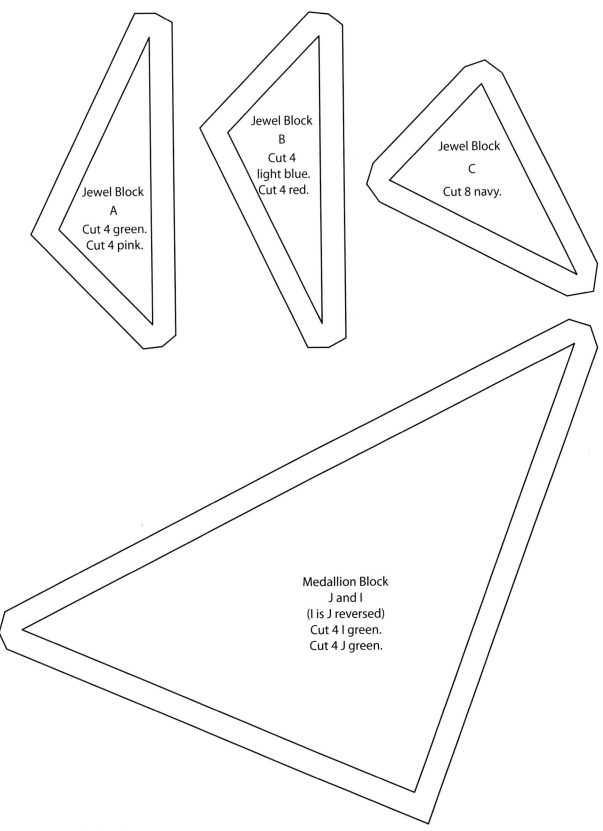

Jewel Block
A
Cut 4 green.
Cut 4 pink.

Jewel Block
B
Cut 4
light blue.
Cut 4 red.

Jewel Block
C
Cut 8 navy.

Medallion Block
J and I
(I is J reversed)
Cut 4 I green.
Cut 4 J green.

crossroads

Finished quilt: *76″ × 76″* • **Finished block:** *12″ × 12″*

design thoughts

Color scheme: This quilt pairs colors from all around the color wheel. Some of the pairs are complements and some aren't, but they all provide enough contrast to make the star stand out from the white background.

Accent color: Black—the black lines ground the design and give it a strong graphic look.

Pieced and machine quilted by **Sandra Clemons**

Design: This quilt reminds me of the open dirt roads in Illinois, where I grew up. During my time in college track, I would go for runs on dirt roads amid cornfields and come to four-way stops, with the same landscape visible in all four directions. The quilt industry has exploded recently with textured fabric, which I love. The tan linen-cotton blend fabric adds subtle depth to the quilt. Some fabrics that aren't 100% cotton can shrink more than cottons do; consider washing everything first if you are going to use a mix of fiber contents.

Hitting your stash and scraps: Make all the large points from a dark print and the pieced points from a light fabric. Or make each star its own color and pick fabrics using the color's tints, tones, and shades (see Thinking About Color, page 5). The possibilities are endless.

Fabric Requirements

White: 1½ yards or 7 fat quarters

Tan: 2¼ yards or 10 fat quarters

Black: 1¾ yards or 8 fat quarters

Scraps: 3 yards of strips— 32 strips need to be at least 1⅞″ × 22″ and 16 strips need to be at least 3″ × 22″

Backing: 5 yards

Batting: 84″ × 84″

Binding: ⅔ yard

Cutting Instructions

To cut the triangles and diamonds for the stars in the Crossroads *block, use Patterns C and D (page 84).*

WHITE

Cut 8 strips 4⅜″ × WOF.

- Subcut into 64 squares 4⅜″ × 4⅜″.
- Cut diagonally once to make 128 A triangles.

Cut 5 strips 3⅜″ × WOF.

- Subcut into 60 squares 3⅜″ × 3⅜″.
- Use the leftover strips from above to cut 4 more squares 3⅜″ × 3⅜″ for a total of 64 squares.
- Cut the squares diagonally once to make 128 B triangles.

TAN

Cut 8 strips 4½″ × WOF.

- Stitch the strips end to end.
- Subcut into 2 pieces 4½″ × 68½″ for side borders.
- Subcut into 2 pieces 4½″ × 76½″ for top and bottom borders.

Cut 14 strips 2½″ × WOF.

Cut 2 strips 2¼″ × WOF.

- Subcut into 25 squares 2¼″ × 2¼″.
- Cut the squares diagonally twice to make 100 quarter-square triangles.

BLACK

Cut 28 strips 1½″ × WOF.

Cut 11 strips 1⅞″ × WOF.

- Subcut into 25 rectangles 1⅞″ × 3″.
- Subcut into 50 rectangles 1⅞″ × 7″.

SCRAPS

Cut 4 triangles of Pattern C from a strip 1⅞″ × 22″. Repeat with 32 strips to make 128 scalene triangles.

Cut 4 diamonds of Pattern D from a strip 3″ × 22″. Repeat with 16 strips to make 64 diamonds.

BINDING

Cut 8 strips 2½″ × WOF.

Block Construction

For some general sewing guidelines, refer to Sewing Notes (page 23). For detailed instructions on pressing in a pinwheel, refer to Special Techniques (page 103).

Crossroads block assembly; make 16.

1. Sew together a Pattern D diamond and a white A triangle. Press the seam toward the D diamond. Make 4. **FIG. A**

2. Sew a white B triangle to the unit from Step 1, offsetting seams as in Step 1. Press the seam toward the half-square triangle. Make 4. **FIG. B**

3. Sew together 2 different Pattern C scalene triangles. Press the seam to one side. Make 4. **FIG. C**

4. Attach a large and small half-square triangle to the unit from Step 3. **FIG. D**

5. Join all 8 units to complete the block. Press the seam in a pinwheel. **FIG. E**

6. Repeat Steps 1–5 to make 16 blocks.

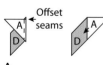

A

B

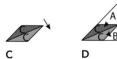

C

D

E

Assemble Cornerstones

Crossroads cornerstone assembly; make 25.

1. Sew a pair of tan quarter-square triangles to both sides of a short black rectangle. Press the seams toward the triangles. Make 50. **FIG. F**

2. Sew 2 of the units from Step 1 to both sides of a long black rectangle. (Before sewing, find the center point of each by folding it in half and finger-pressing a crease. Match up the creases before stitching.) Press the seams toward the black fabric. Make 25. **FIG.G**

3. Trim the block to a 4½˝ × 4½˝ square. **FIG. H**

F

G

H

Assemble Sashings

Crossroads sashing unit assembly; make 40.

1. Strip piece 2 black 1½˝-wide fabric strips to each side of the 2½˝-wide tan fabric strip. Press the seams toward the tan fabric.

2. Subcut the units from Step 1 into segments 12½˝ long. Make 40.

Assemble Quilt Top

Crossroads **quilt assembly**

1. Arrange the cornerstones, sashing, and blocks as shown in the *Crossroads* quilt assembly diagram.

2. Make the rows first by sewing together the sashing units and the cornerstones and sewing together the sashing units and the blocks. Press all the seams toward the sashing.

3. Sew together the rows to make the quilt center. Press the seams toward the sashing.

4. Attach the side borders first and then the top and bottom borders. Press the seams toward the borders.

Finish Quilt

For instructions on quilt finishing, refer to Quiltmaking Basics (page 109).

1. Prepare and layer the quilt top, batting, and backing.

2. Quilt as desired.

3. Bind the quilt.

4. Add a label.

OPTION: crossroads wallhanging

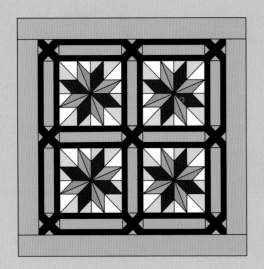

Finished wallhanging: 44″ × 44″
Finished block: 12″ × 12″

For a smaller wallhanging version of Crossroads, substitute the following fabric requirements and cutting instructions and refer to the Crossroads wallhanging assembly diagram for placement. Follow all the construction and assembly directions for the main quilt, beginning at Block Construction (page 81).

Fabric Requirements

White: ¼ yard or 2 fat quarters

Gray: ¼ yard or 2 fat quarters

Lavender: 1 yard or 5 fat quarters

Black: ½ yard or 3 fat quarters

Navy: 1 fat quarter

Orange: 1 fat quarter

Green: 1 fat quarter

Backing: 2½ yards

Batting: 52″ × 52″

Binding: ½ yard

Cutting Instructions

WHITE

Cut 1 strip 4⅜″ × WOF.

- Subcut into 8 squares 4⅜″ × 4⅜″.
- Cut diagonally once to make 16 A triangles.

Cut 1 strip 3⅜″ × WOF.

- Subcut into 8 squares 3⅜″ × 3⅜″.
- Cut the squares diagonally once to make 16 B triangles.

GRAY

Cut 1 strip 4⅜″ × WOF.

- Subcut into 8 squares 4⅜″ × 4⅜″.
- Cut the squares diagonally once to make 16 A triangles.

Cut 1 strip 3⅜″ × WOF.

- Subcut into 8 squares 3⅜″ × 3⅜″.
- Cut the squares diagonally once to make 16 B triangles.

LAVENDER

Cut 5 strips 4½″ × WOF for the border.

- Stitch the strips end to end.
- Subcut into 2 pieces 4½″ × 36½″ for side borders.
- Subcut into 2 pieces 4½″ × 44½″ for top and bottom borders.

Cut 4 strips 2½″ × WOF.

Cut 1 strip 2¼″ × WOF.

- Subcut into 9 squares 2¼″ × 2¼″.
- Cut the squares diagonally twice to make 36 quarter-square triangles.

BLACK

Cut 8 strips 1½″ × WOF.

Cut 3 strips 1⅞″ × WOF.

- Subcut into 18 rectangles 1⅞″ × 3″.
- Subcut into 9 rectangles 1⅞″ × 7″.

NAVY

Cut 16 diamonds using Pattern D.

ORANGE

Cut 4 triangles of Pattern C from a strip 1⅞″ × 22″. Repeat to make 16 scalene triangles.

GREEN

Cut 4 triangles of Pattern C from a strip 1⅞″ × 22″. Repeat to make 16 scalene triangles.

BINDING

Cut 5 strips 2½″ × WOF.

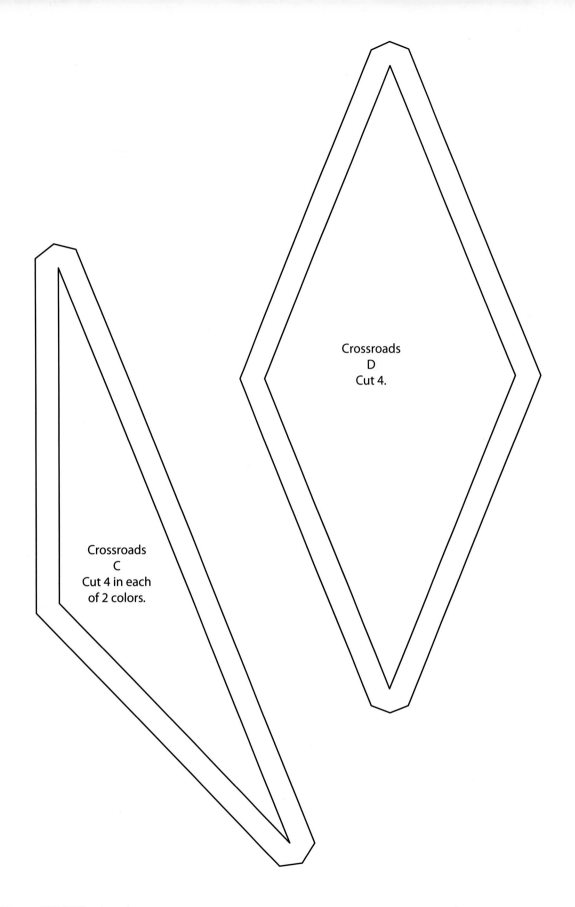

Crossroads
D
Cut 4.

Crossroads
C
Cut 4 in each
of 2 colors.

magic

Finished quilt: 48″ × 48″ • **Finished block:** 12″ × 12″

design thoughts

Color scheme: Triadic, using blue, yellow, and tints and tones of red for a sophisticated color scheme (see Color Relationships, page 7).

Accent color: White—the white print frames the stars, highlighting a starry secondary pattern.

Design: Using black in contrast to the pink and yellow gives this quilt a balance of hardness and softness. There are a lot of inspiring black prints on the market today.

Hitting your stash and scraps: Use a variety of darks for the black, lights for the whites and blues, and mediums in place of yellow and pink if you want to change the color scheme but keep the same balance.

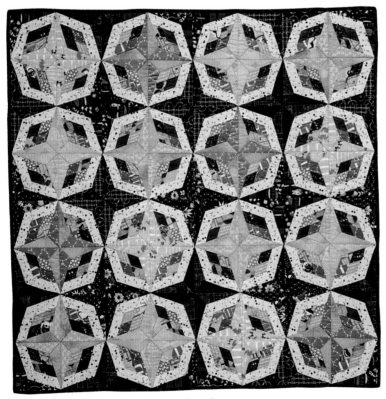

Pieced and machine quilted by Sandra Clemons

Fabric Requirements

Black: 4 fat quarters

Pink: 4 fat quarters

Gray: 4 fat quarters

Yellow: 4 fat quarters

White: 1 yard or 5 fat quarters

Scraps: 1 yard total for diamonds

Backing: 3 yards

Batting: 56″ × 56″

Binding: ½ yard

Cutting Instructions

To cut the triangles and diamonds, use Patterns A, B, and C (page 90).

BLACK AND PINK

From each fat quarter, cut 4 strips 2⅛″ × 18″.

- Subcut each strip into 4 scalene triangles using Pattern A. Cut 16 from each fat quarter.

GRAY AND YELLOW

From each fat quarter, cut 4 strips 2⅛″ × 18″.

- Subcut each strip into 4 scalene triangles using Pattern B. Cut 16 from each fat quarter.

WHITE

Cut 18 strips 1¾″ × WOF.

- Subcut into 320 diamonds using Pattern C.

SCRAPS

Cut scraps into strips 1¾″ × WOF.

- Subcut into 256 diamonds using Pattern C.

BINDING

Cut 5 strips 2½″ × WOF.

Block Construction

For some general sewing guidelines, refer to Sewing Notes (page 23). For detailed instructions on sewing Y-seams and pressing in a pinwheel, refer to Special Techniques (page 103).

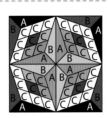

Magic block assembly; make 16

1. Make large pieced diamonds by sewing together rows of smaller scalene diamonds as shown in the *Magic* block assembly diagram. There are 3 rows with 3 diamonds in each row. Start with row 1 and sew together 3 white diamonds. Sew together rows 2 and 3 following a white-scrap-scrap pattern. Press seams to the left on the top and bottom rows. Press seams to the right on the middle row and to the left on the bottom row. **FIG. A**

2. Sew together the rows to form a large pieced diamond. **FIG. B**

3. Repeat Steps 1 and 2 to make 64 large diamonds. **FIG. C**

4. Sew together a gray scalene triangle and a large diamond as shown. Do not press yet.

TIP

The notch of the triangle fits into the corner of the diamond.

Match notch.

A   B   C

5. Sew the black scalene triangle to the diamond unit with a Y-seam. Press the seam between the gray and black fabrics toward the gray fabric and the seam between the large diamond and the scalene triangle toward the triangle. **FIG. D**

D

6. Repeat Step 5, attaching the pink and yellow scalene triangles to the remaining sides of the big diamond.

7. Complete the block by sewing together the units. Press the seam in a pinwheel. **FIG. E**

8. Repeat Steps 1–7 to make 16 blocks.

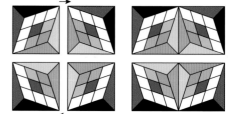

E

Assemble Quilt Top

Magic **quilt assembly**

1. Arrange the pieces as shown in the *Magic* quilt assembly diagram.

2. Sew together the blocks to make rows. Press the seams open.

3. Stitch together the rows. Press the seams open.

Finish Quilt

For instructions on quilt finishing, refer to Quiltmaking Basics (page 109).

1. Prepare and layer the quilt top, batting, and backing.

2. Quilt as desired.

3. Bind the quilt.

4. Add a label.

ALTERNATIVE COLOR SCHEME

Put a different spell on Magic by changing the color scheme. This one features purple, pink, and green and includes a 4˝ border.

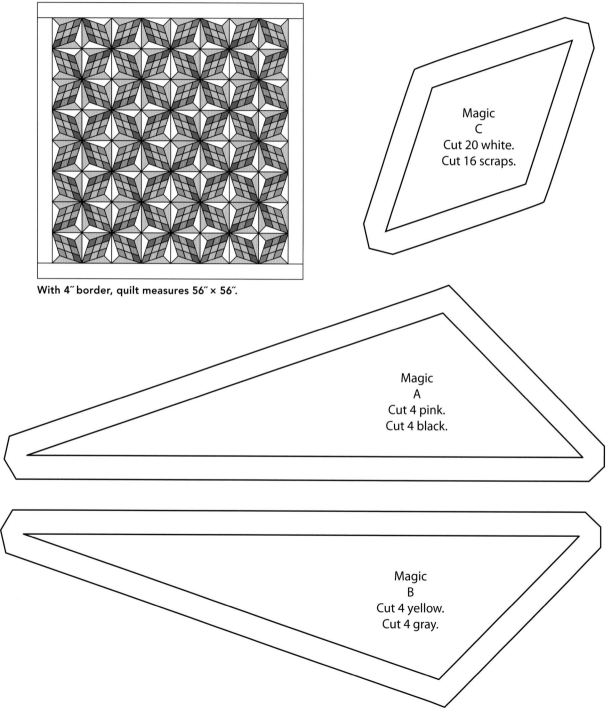

With 4˝ border, quilt measures 56˝ × 56˝.

Magic
C
Cut 20 white.
Cut 16 scraps.

Magic
A
Cut 4 pink.
Cut 4 black.

Magic
B
Cut 4 yellow.
Cut 4 gray.

film

Finished quilt: 57˝ × 74¾˝ • **Finished block:** 14˝ × 14˝

Pieced and machine quilted by Sandra Clemons

design thoughts

Color scheme: Rainbow colors are made brighter by the white that surrounds them.

Accent color: Black—the black squares provide depth as well as a graphic feel.

Design: I enjoy photography and love to go outside to take pictures. This quilt reminds me of film—from the predigital days.

Hitting your stash and scraps: Try medium to dark scraps in place of the black squares in the sashing and low-volume prints to really make the sashing scrappy. Pick colors in a split-complementary color scheme (see Exciting Color Schemes, page 10). Make each block with all three of the colors and repeat to make all the blocks.

Fabric Requirements

Ivory: 2 yards
  or 9 fat quarters

White: ⅞ yard
  or 4 fat quarters

Black: ⅝ yard
  or 3 fat quarters

Gray: ⅞ yard
  or 4 fat quarters

Scraps: 2 yards total—
  12 light fabrics at least
  8˝ × 12˝ and 12 dark
  fabrics at least 10˝ × 10˝

Backing: 3½ yards

Batting: 65˝ × 83˝

Binding: ⅔ yard

Cutting Instructions

IVORY

Cut 5 strips 1¾" × WOF.

Cut 8 strips 1¾" × WOF.
- Subcut into 186 squares 1¾" × 1¾".

Cut 3 strips 14½" × WOF.
- Subcut into 62 strips 1¾" × 14½".

WHITE

Cut 5 strips 4¾" × WOF.
- Subcut into 96 rectangles 1⅞" × 4¾".

BLACK

Cut 11 strips 1¾" × WOF.
- Subcut 7 strips into 155 squares 1¾" × 1¾".

GRAY

Cut 1 strip 12½" × WOF.
- Subcut into 24 strips 1½" × 12½".

Cut 1 strip 14½" × WOF.
- Subcut into 24 strips 1½" × 14½".

SCRAPS

From each light fabric:

Cut 2 squares 3⅞" × 3⅞".
- Cut each square diagonally once to make 4 half-square triangles.

Cut 1 square 7¼" × 7¼".
- Cut the square diagonally twice to make 4 quarter-square triangles.

From each dark fabric:

Cut 4 rectangles 1⅞" × 4¾".

Cut 1 square 4¾" × 4¾".

BINDING

Cut 7 strips 2½" × WOF.

Block Construction

For some general sewing guidelines, refer to Sewing Notes (page 23).

Film block assembly; make 12.

1. Sew 2 white rectangles to each side of a dark fabric rectangle. Make 4. **FIG. A**

A

2. Stitch 2 units from Step 1 to each side of a dark square. **FIG. B**

B

3. Stitch a light fabric quarter-square triangle to each side of the 2 remaining units from Step 1. **FIG. C**

C

4. Join the units from Steps 2 and 3. Press as indicated. Complete the block by sewing light fabric half-square triangles to the outside corners of the block. **FIG. D**

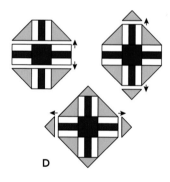

D

5. Add the gray frame around the block. Stitch the side logs to the block and then add the top and bottom logs. **FIG. E**

E

6. Repeat Steps 1–5 to make 12 blocks.

Assemble Pieced Sashing Corners

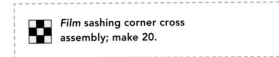 *Film* sashing corner cross assembly; make 20.

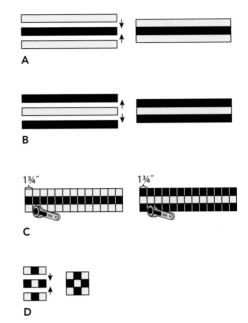

A

B

C

D

1. Sew 2 ivory strips to either side of a black strip. Make 2. **FIG. A**

2. Sew 2 black strips to either side of an ivory strip. **FIG. B**

3. Subcut the units made in Steps 1 and 2 into pieces 1¾″. Make 40 ivory-black-ivory pieces and 20 black-ivory-black pieces. **FIG. C**

4. Sew together the pieces to make Nine-Patches with a cross shape. The block finishes at 3¾″ × 3¾″. Make 20. **FIG. D**

Assemble Pieced Sashing

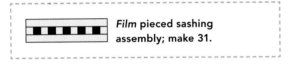 *Film* pieced sashing assembly; make 31.

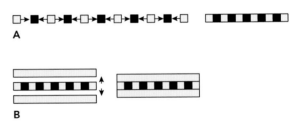

A

B

1. Sew together a row of 5 black squares and 6 ivory squares, alternating the colors and starting with an ivory square. **FIG. A**

2. Stitch 2 ivory logs on each side of the row from Step 1. Make 31. **FIG. B**

Assemble Quilt Top

Film **quilt assembly**

1. Arrange the quilt top as shown in the *Film* quilt assembly diagram.

2. Assemble the rows first by sewing together the sashing units and the cornerstones and then sewing together the sashing units and the blocks. Press all the seams toward the sashing.

3. Stitch together the rows and press the seams in one direction.

Finish Quilt

For instructions on quilt finishing, refer to Quiltmaking Basics (page 109).

1. Prepare and layer the quilt top, batting, and backing.

2. Quilt as desired.

3. Bind the quilt.

4. Add a label.

OPTION: film wallhanging

Finished wallhanging: 40″ × 40″
Finished block: 14″ × 14″

For a smaller wallhanging version of Film, *substitute the following fabric requirements and cutting instructions and refer to the* Film *wallhanging assembly diagram for placement. Follow all the construction and assembly directions for the main quilt, beginning at Block Construction (page 92).*

Fabric Requirement

Lavender: 1¼ yards or 6 fat quarters

White: ⅓ yard or 2 fat quarters

Navy: ⅓ yard or 2 fat quarters

Yellow: ⅓ yard or 2 fat quarters

Backing: 2 yards

Batting: 48″ × 48″

Binding: ⅓ yard

Cutting Instructions

LAVENDER

Cut 6 strips 4½″ × WOF for borders and sashing.

- Subcut 3 strips into pieces 4½″ × 32½″ for side borders and middle sashing.
- Subcut 2 strips into pieces 4½″ × 40½″ for top and bottom borders.
- Subcut 1 strip into 2 sashing units 4½″ × 14½″.

Cut 1 strip 3⅞″ × WOF.

- Subcut into 8 squares 3⅞″ × 3⅞″.

- Cut each square diagonally once to make 16 half-square triangles.

Cut 1 strip 7¼″ × WOF.

- Subcut into 4 squares 7¼″ × 7¼″.
- Cut each square diagonally twice to make 16 quarter-square triangles.

WHITE

Cut 2 strips 4¾″ × WOF.

- Subcut into 32 rectangles 1⅞″ × 4¾″.

NAVY

Cut 6 strips 1½″ × WOF.

Cut 8 logs 1½″ × 12½″.

Cut 8 logs 1½″ × 14½″.

YELLOW

Cut 2 strips 4¾″ × WOF.

- Subcut into 16 rectangles 1⅞″ × 4¾″.
- Subcut into 4 squares 4¾″ × 4¾″.

BINDING

Cut 4 strips 2½″ × WOF.

slide

Finished quilt: 68″ × 84″ • **Finished block:** 12″ × 12″

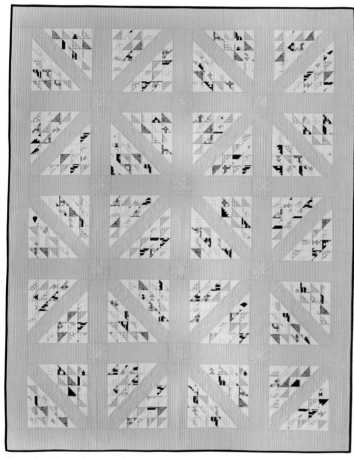

Pieced and machine quilted by Sandra Clemons

design thoughts

<u>Color scheme:</u> This harmonious, low-volume quilt actually has a complementary color scheme (blue and orange). It shows the power of using tints and tones for variety.

<u>Accent color:</u> Seafoam—the pale blue-green stars highlight the warm sashing.

<u>Design:</u> This is a great example of a low-volume quilt that is still strong and graphic.

<u>Hitting your scraps and stash:</u> Replace the white yardage with low-volume prints. Or do you like more traditional color schemes? Make this with a complementary color scheme in yellow and purple. Make the sashing purple, the stars yellow, and scrap in the half-square triangles (see Color Relationships, page 7).

Fabric Requirements

Coral: 3⅔ yards or 16 fat quarters

Seafoam: ¼ yard or 2 fat quarters

White: 2 yards or 9 fat quarters

Scraps: 1½ yards total

Backing: 5 yards

Batting: 76″ × 92″

Binding: ¾ yard

Cutting Instructions

CORAL

Cut 8 strips 4½″ × WOF for borders.

- Stitch the strips end to end.
- Subcut 2 pieces 4½″ × 76½″ for side borders.
- Subcut 2 pieces 4½″ × 68½″ for top and bottom borders.

Cut 11 strips 4½″ × WOF.

- Subcut into 31 sashing rectangles 4½″ × 12½″.

Cut 1 strip 3¼″ × WOF.

- Subcut into 12 squares 3¼″ × 3¼″.
- Cut each square diagonally twice to total 48 quarter-square triangles.

Cut 2 strips 1½″ × WOF.

- Subcut into 48 squares 1½″ × 1½″.

Cut 10 strips 3⅜″ × WOF.

- Subcut into 20 block rectangles 3⅜″ × 18″.

SEAFOAM

Cut 1 strip 2½″ × WOF.

- Subcut into 12 squares 2½″ × 2½″.

Cut 2 strips 1⅞″ × WOF.

- Subcut into 48 squares 1⅞″ × 1⅞″. Use the leftovers from the 2½″ strip to achieve 48 squares.
- Cut each square diagonally once to total 96 quarter-square triangles.

WHITE

Cut 22 strips 2⅞″ × WOF.

- Subcut into 300 squares 2⅞″ × 2⅞″.
- Cut each square diagonally once to total 600 half-square triangles.

SCRAPS

Cut 200 squares 2⅞″ × 2⅞″.

- Cut each square diagonally once to total 400 half-square triangles.

BINDING

Cut 8 strips 2½″ × WOF.

Block Construction

For some general sewing guidelines, refer to Sewing Notes (page 23). For detailed instructions on making half-square triangles, refer to Special Techniques (page 103).

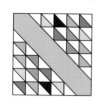

Slide block assembly; make 20.

1. Sew 20 scrap and 20 white half-square triangles together to make 20 triangle square units per block. Press seam allowances toward the scrap fabrics. **FIG. A**

2. Sew the triangle square units into rows with 5 white half-square triangles and then sew the rows together. Press the seam allowances as shown. Repeat to make 2 scrappy triangles. **FIG. B**

3. Sew 2 scrappy triangles to each side of a coral block rectangle. (Before sewing, find the center point of each by folding it in half and finger-pressing a crease. Match up the creases before stitching.) Press the seams toward the coral fabric and trim the block to 12½˝ × 12½˝. **FIG. C**

4. Repeat Steps 1–3 to make 20 blocks.

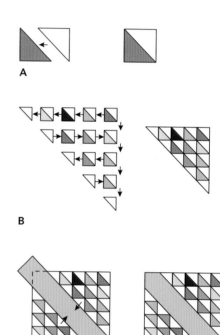

A

B

C

Sashing Block Construction

For detailed instructions on making Flying Geese, refer to Special Techniques (page 103).

 Slide sashing block assembly; **make 12.**

1. Sew together 2 seafoam triangles and 1 coral triangle to make a Flying Geese unit. The corners of the small triangles will extend ¼˝ beyond each end of the large triangle, creating an offset seam and dog-ears. Press seams toward the half-square triangles and trim the dog-ears. Repeat to make 4. **FIG. D**

2. Sew coral squares to 2 of the Flying Geese. **FIG. E**

3. Sew the remaining 2 Flying Geese to either side of the seafoam 2½˝ × 2½˝ square. **FIG. F**

4. Complete the block according to the assembly diagram. **FIG. G**

5. Repeat Steps 1–4 to make 12 blocks.

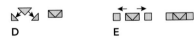

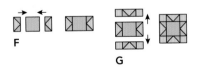

Assemble Quilt Top

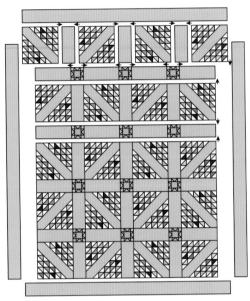

Slide quilt assembly

1. Arrange the sashing and blocks as shown in the *Slide* quilt assembly diagram.

2. Sew together the sashing pieces and the blocks to form rows, pressing the seams toward the sashing.

3. Sew together the rows to make the quilt center, pressing the seams in one direction.

4. Attach the side borders first and then attach the top and bottom borders. Press the seams toward the borders.

Finish Quilt

For instructions on quilt finishing, refer to Quiltmaking Basics (page 109).

1. Prepare and layer the quilt top, batting, and backing.

2. Quilt as desired.

3. Bind the quilt.

4. Add a label.

OPTION: slide wallhanging

Finished wallhanging: 36″ × 36″
Finished block: 12″ × 12″

For a smaller wallhanging version of Slide, substitute the following fabric requirements and cutting instructions and refer to the Slide wallhanging assembly diagram for placement. Follow all the construction and assembly directions for the main quilt, beginning at Block Construction (page 99).

Fabric Requirements

Purple: 1 yard or 5 fat quarters

Green: small scrap

White: ½ yard or 3 fat quarters

Other scraps: ¼ yard total

Backing: 1¼ yards

Binding: ⅓ yard

Cutting Instructions

PURPLE

Cut 4 strips 4½″ × WOF.

- Cut 2 pieces 4½″ × 28½″ for side borders.
- Cut 2 pieces 4½″ × 36½″ for top and bottom borders.

Cut 2 strips 4½″ × WOF.

- Subcut into 4 sashing rectangles 4½″ × 12½″.
- Cut 1 square 3¼″ × 3¼″ from leftover fabric.
- Cut the square diagonally twice to make 4 quarter-square triangles.

Cut 4 squares 1½″ × 1½″.

Cut 2 strips ⅜″ × WOF.

- Subcut into 4 block rectangles 3⅜″ × 18″.

GREEN

Cut 1 square 2½″ × 2½″.

- Cut 4 squares 1⅞″ × 1⅞″.
- Cut each square diagonally once to make 8 half-square triangles.

WHITE

Cut 5 strips 2⅞″ × WOF.

- Subcut into 60 squares 2⅞″ × 2⅞″.
- Cut each square diagonally once to make 120 half-square triangles.

FAT QUARTERS

Cut 40 squares 2⅞″ × 2⅞″.

- Cut each square diagonally once to make 80 half-square triangles.

BINDING

Cut 4 strips 2½″ × WOF.

SPECIAL TECHNIQUES

Cutting Strips

The patterns in this book require you to cut a lot of strips and to subcut those strips into squares, half-square triangles, and quarter-square triangles.

Do not rely on the grid lines on a cutting mat for measuring. Instead, use the lines on a gridded ruler because they are more accurate. The lines on a mat are useful for straightening out fabric before cutting and for double-checking cuts.

SUBCUTTING STRIPS INTO SQUARES

Once the strips are cut, stack four layers, using the grid lines on your cutting mat as a guide for lining up the strips. Use a rotary cutter and an acrylic ruler to cut the strips into squares. As you gain more experience, try adding a few more layers.

CUTTING SQUARES DIAGONALLY

If the cutting instructions tell you to cut diagonally (once or twice), you will be cutting triangles.

Half-Square Triangles

To cut once diagonally, find the 45° angle line on your ruler and place it over one of the cut sides of the squares. Make sure that the ruler sits right on the corners; then cut, making two half-square triangles.

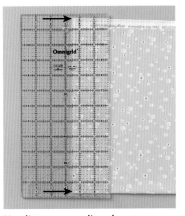

Use lines on acrylic rulers to measure cuts.

TIP

Accurate Cutting

Accuracy is extremely important when cutting because inaccuracies can compound as you work through the construction process. When lining up fabric with the grid lines on a ruler, aim for the center of the line and stick with one brand of rulers.

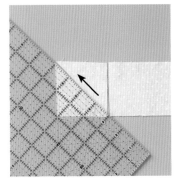

Quarter-Square Triangles

Use the same technique to make quarter-square triangles by cutting twice diagonally, creating four triangles. Use the 45° line on your ruler for both cuts.

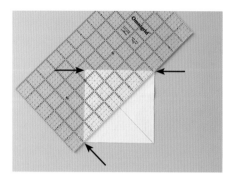

USING TEMPLATES

Pattern pieces are used for shapes that are not easily cut with a rotary cutter. Quilters often trace pattern pieces onto clear plastic to make templates. However, I prefer to use templates in a different way.

1. Photocopy the template. Make sure there is no print scaling. Cut out the template with scissors. The cutting instructions will direct you to cut fabric strips of a particular width to use with each template.

2. Place the paper template along the strip. Align the ruler on top of the template. Make sure the ¼˝ line of the ruler matches the ¼˝ line on the template.

3. Align the 45° angle line on the ruler with the bottom of the strip. Cut to the right of the template.

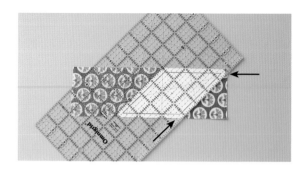

TIP

Templates must be accurate because errors will compound with each step. Check your accuracy by making a test block before cutting up all the fabric for your quilt.

4. Without moving the fabric strip, rotate the paper template 180° and align the template with the previous cut. Cut again. Continue rotating and cutting to the end of the strip.

5. Cut out the notches shown on the pattern.

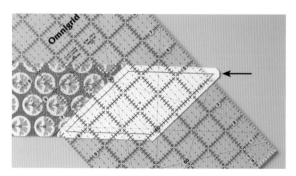

TIP

Cutting Mistakes

There may be times when you mess up on your cuts. Take a breath and assess the damage. Maybe you can use the messed-up cuts for other pieces. If you are short on fabric as a result and can't replace the print, maybe it's time to add an entirely new fabric to the quilt. Mistakes do happen, but as you get more experience, they are usually less frequent and less costly.

Locking Seams

When seams meet in patchwork, they often need to match precisely for the design to look right. The project instructions specify in which direction to press seam allowances to reduce bulk and to ensure that intersecting seams will lock.

Pin together seams to help keep the pieces aligned as you sew. As you gain more experience and build confidence, you'll need to pin less.

As you sew, the seam on the top unit should fold away from you and the bottom unit should have the seam facing toward you. As the unit goes through the machine, the machine will slightly push the top unit into the bottom unit's seam, locking the seam.

Pressing in a Pinwheel

Place your work wrong side up on the pressing surface. Flatten center seam by creating a small pinwheel where all the seams rotate in a clockwise direction.

Flying Geese

Many of the patterns in this book include Flying Geese units. It is common to create these blocks by joining a rectangle and two squares. But that method requires extra trimming and creates waste.

Instead, I use two half-square triangles and a quarter-square triangle to make a Flying Geese unit. (To make half- and quarter-square triangles, refer to Cutting Squares Diagonally, page 103.)

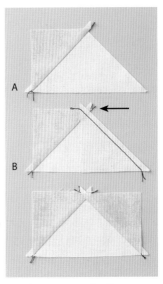

1. With right sides together, sew a half-square triangle to a quarter-square triangle. Press the seam in the direction stated in the project. **FIG. A**

2. Add the other half-square triangle to the other side of the unit. Note that the triangles are aligned along the bottom of the unit and another dog-ear forms at the top. Press the seam toward the half-square triangle (unless directed otherwise in the project). **FIG. B**

Square-in-a-Square

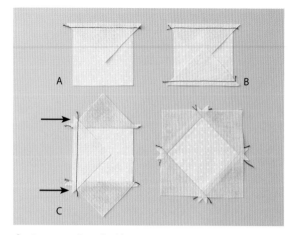

1. Start with 4 half-square triangles and a square to make a square-in-a-square. Fold the square in half and finger-press along the edge to create a crease. Repeat on the long side of the triangles. Open up all pieces.

2. Match creases from the triangle and the square formed in Step 1 and sew triangle. Notice that there are dog-ears. Press the seam away from the square. **FIG. A**

3. Add another triangle directly across from the first triangle as directed in Step 2. **FIG. B**

4. Attach the remaining triangles as directed in Step 2. **FIG. C**

Chain Piecing

Chain piecing is the fastest way to sew together a lot of pieces.

Make a pile of matched pieces that are ready to be sewn. Stitch the first pair; then, without cutting the thread or lifting the presser foot, sew a few stitches with no fabric underneath the foot, insert the next set of pieces under the foot, and continue sewing. You will form a "chain" of pieced sets.

Continue until the pile is complete. Then snip apart the pieces.

Strip Piecing

After cutting strips of fabric, stitch them together lengthwise and then subcut the strip units into smaller pieces.

When making a stripped set, make sure the pieces of fabric are aligned. After sewing together two strips, press the seam to one side. If you plan to add another strip, it's helpful to sew it to the unit in the opposite direction to ensure the stripped unit is evenly stitched and not pulling too much in one direction.

When subcutting strip units, use the grid lines on a cutting mat and the grid lines on a transparent ruler for accuracy. Align the piece along a grid line on the mat and check that the other side of the piece also follows a line. Use a ruler to subcut the units, checking that the lines on the ruler hit the seams along the stripped piece at the same measurement on ruler.

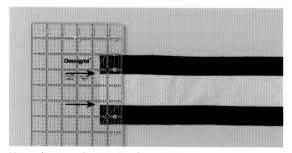

Use ruler to subcut units from strip set.

Dog-Ears

Dog-ears are small fabric corners that protrude after sewing together pieces with diagonal sides, such as triangles. Unless the dog-ears will show through a light-colored fabric on the finished quilt top, I don't take the time to trim them away. But the choice is yours.

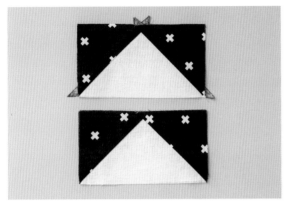

Untrimmed and trimmed dog-ears

Y-Seams

When three pieces of fabric come together at a single point, a Y-seam occurs—the seams form a Y shape. You need to be precise when sewing these seams.

1. Sew together 2 of the pieces, right sides together. Do not press the seam yet. Pull out 1 to 2 stitches from one end of the seam. (You could stop stitching ¼″ from the top and backstitch, but I don't since I'm usually chain piecing.)

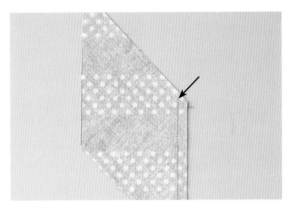

2. Take the third piece of fabric and begin by stitching it to the left side of the unit with the seam facing you. Sew right up to the seam, but don't stitch over it. You should be ¼″ from the end of the third piece. Stop. Lift the presser foot and the needle.

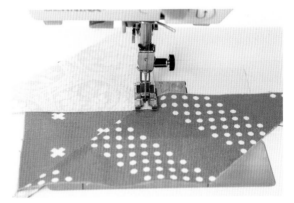

3. Rotate the third fabric to finish up the seam. Don't cut the thread. Fold over the seam away from you. Maneuver the third piece so that it aligns with the fabric underneath. This means that not only are your second and third fabrics aligned but also your first and second fabrics are aligned on top of each other, while your third fabric is rolled over itself with the right side on the inside of the roll.

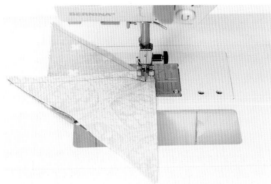

4. Put the presser foot down and drop the needle so it lands close to the seam but doesn't hit it. Stitch through the rest of the way.

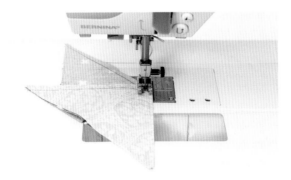

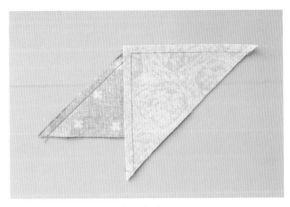

There are two methods for pressing a Y-seam. Either press in a pinwheel or press the first seam to one side and then press the Y-shaped seam.

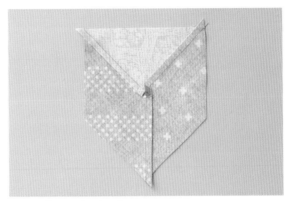

Pressed as a pinwheel

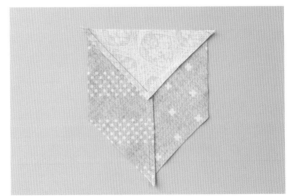

Pressed to one side

QUILTMAKING BASICS: HOW TO FINISH YOUR QUILT

Quilting

Quilting, whether by hand or machine, enhances the quilt's pieced or appliquéd design. You may choose to quilt-in-the-ditch, echo the pieced or appliquéd motifs, use patterns from quilting design books and stencils, or do your own free-motion quilting. Remember to check your batting manufacturer's recommendations for how close the quilting lines must be.

Binding

Trim excess batting and backing from the quilt so it is even with the edges of the quilt top.

DOUBLE-FOLD STRAIGHT-GRAIN BINDING

If you want a ¼˝ finished binding, cut the binding strips 2˝ wide and piece them together with diagonal seams to make a continuous binding strip. Trim the seam allowance to ¼˝. Press the seams open.

TIP

Pieced Binding

Don't overlook the impact that an awesome binding can have on your quilt. Perhaps your quilt warrants a nice scrappy binding. Before attaching a multicolored binding, audition it around your quilt to check that you like the way the colors land.

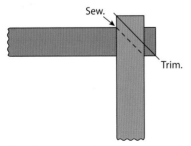

Sew.

Trim.

Sew from corner to corner.

Completed diagonal seam

Press the entire strip in half lengthwise with wrong sides together. With raw edges even, pin the binding to the quilt's front edge a few inches from a corner; leave the first few inches of the binding unattached. Start sewing, using a ¼˝ seam allowance.

Stop ¼˝ away from the first corner (see Step 1) and backstitch one stitch. Lift the presser foot and the needle. Rotate the quilt one-quarter. Fold the binding at a right angle so it extends straight above the quilt and the fold forms a 45° angle in the corner (see Step 2). Bring the binding strip down so it is even with the edge of the quilt (see Step 3). Begin sewing at the folded edge. Repeat in the same manner at all corners.

Continue stitching until you are back near the beginning of the binding strip. See Finishing the Binding Ends (below).

FINISHING THE BINDING ENDS

Refer to ctpub.com > Quiltmaking Basics and Sewing Tips > Completing a Binding with an Invisible Seam.

Fold the ending tail of the binding back on itself where it meets the beginning binding tail. From the fold, measure and mark the cut width of your binding strip. Cut the ending binding tail to this measurement. For example, if your binding is cut 2⅛˝ wide, measure from the fold on the ending tail of the binding 2⅛˝ and cut the binding tail to this length.

Open both tails. Place one tail on top of the other tail at right angles, right sides together. Mark a diagonal line from corner to corner and stitch on the line. Check that you've done it correctly and that the binding fits the quilt; then trim the seam allowance to ¼˝. Press open.

Refold the binding and stitch this binding section in place on the quilt. Fold the binding over the raw edges to the quilt back and hand stitch.

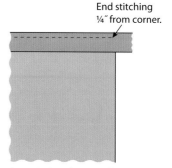

Step 1. Stitch to ¼˝ from corner.

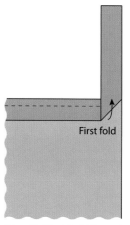

Step 2. First fold for miter

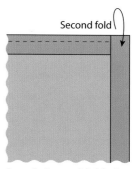

Step 3. Second fold alignment

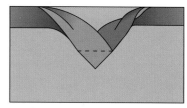

Stitch ends of binding diagonally.

About the Author

SANDRA CLEMONS began sewing at a young age with her mom and has been quilting since 2004. Her quilts have been published in numerous quilting magazines, including *Modern Quilts Unlimited*, *McCall's Quilting*, *American Patchwork & Quilting*, *Quiltmaker*, and *Quilts and More*. *Scrap Patchwork* is Sandra's first book.

Sandra enjoys teaching classes, giving lectures to quilt guilds, and retreating with quilters. She holds a bachelor's degree in finance from Northern Illinois University and a master's degree in business administration from Benedictine University. Sandra lives in Denver, Colorado, with her husband and daughter. Find her online at sandraclemons.blogspot.com.

Suppliers and Manufacturers

I'm so grateful to have worked with the following companies. Without their generosity, I wouldn't be able to afford the publication of my first book.

American Made Brand
americanmadebrand.com

Andover Fabrics   andoverfabrics.com

Art Gallery Fabrics   artgalleryfabrics.com

Aurifil Threads   aurifil.com

C&T Publishing, Inc.   ctpub.com

Dear Stella Design   dearstelladesign.com

The Electric Quilt
Company   electricquilt.com

FreeSpirit Fabric   freespiritfabric.com

Michael Miller Fabrics
michaelmillerfabrics.com

Moda Fabrics   unitednotions.com

Pellon   pellonprojects.com

Riley Blake Designs   rileyblakedesigns.com

RJR Fabrics   rjrfabrics.com

Rowan Fabric   westminsterfabrics.com

The Stencil Company   quiltingstencils.com

The Warm Company   warmcompany.com

Windham Fabrics   windhamfabrics.com